FASHION WATERCOLOR illustration

How to Paint Stylish Compositions

— from Street to Interiors

by Anna Nadler

ISBN: 9781958428436

Table of Contents

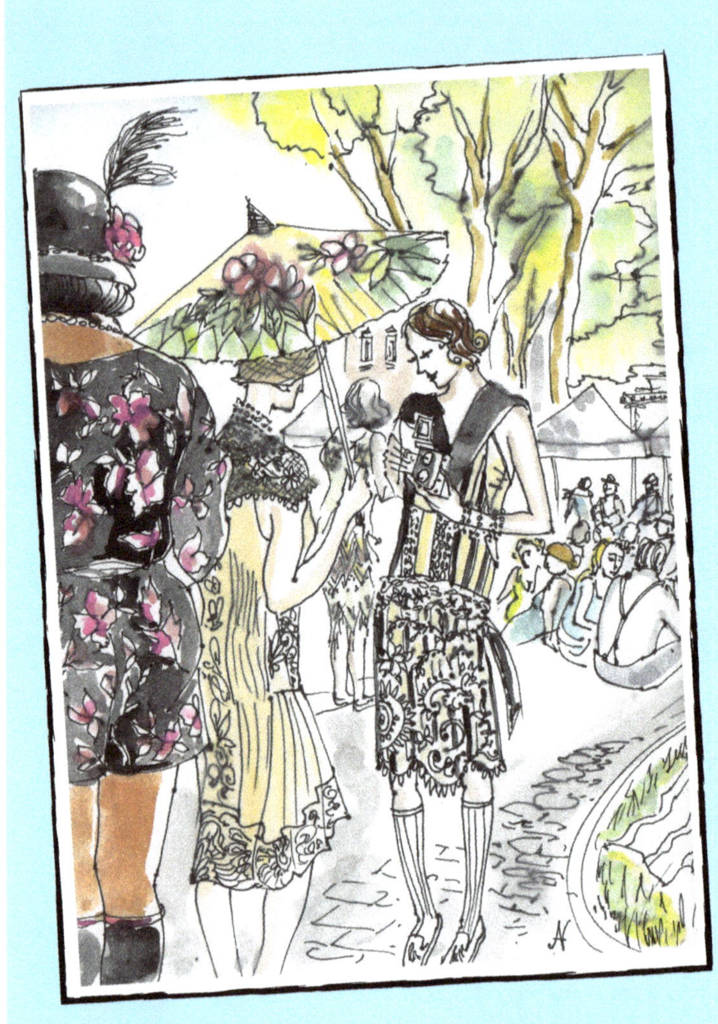

Dear fashion illustration lover, welcome to this new volume.

This book is all about building upon what you have already learned, to create fabulous fashion art within a scene.
It can also serve as a reference book for all levels of skill, as it features many painting examples – to inspire you.

To familiarize yourself with the basics of watercolor painting, I recommend first reading my book "Fashion Illustration Techniques in Watercolor."

This book is packed with simple step by step exercises to help guide you through the process of creating dynamic and interesting compositions, of one, two, three or more fashion figures, with simple and complex backgrounds. Backgrounds can feature nature, cityscapes, interiors, and more. We will go over the rules of one and two point perspective, fashion figure basics, as well as using colors. While this book focuses on watercolor, we will also explore using other media, like markers and artist pens.

Once you understand the relationship of the figure to its surroundings and other figures, you will be able to use photo references to create your own watercolor fashion compositions.

We will jump from simple and loose illustration to drawing from photo references, then back to loose illustration. As a versatile artist, you should learn to do both. If later on you only want to stick to realism or loose art, it is up to you.

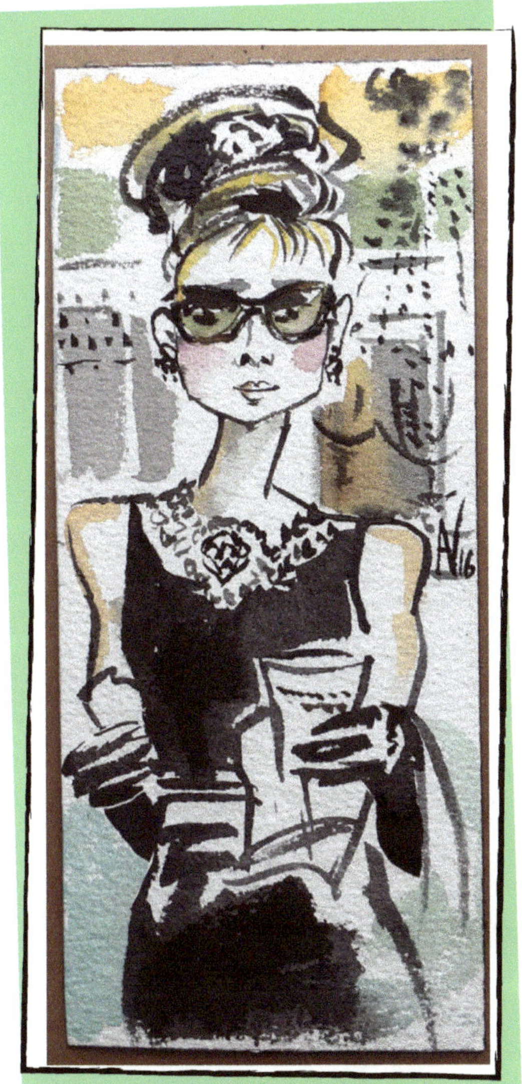

This book will encourage you to dare and experiment, to be bold and brave in your fashion artwork.

Ever wanted to try drawing live, on location? This book will also touch on creating cool art on your travels and give you ideas on portable and convenient art supplies to get for that purpose.

Finally, this book will teach you to use your own imagination, combined with references to make unique and fun fashion compositions.

Some exercises in this book use only watercolor, some use watercolor combined with pens and/or markers. It is up to you whether you want to use one or all of these in any given exercise in this book.

The ultimate goal of this volume is to have as much fun as possible, while honing your skills with tenacity and consistency.

This book is the next step to transitioning from a beginner to advanced fashion watercolor artist.

Let us embark on this fun adventure!

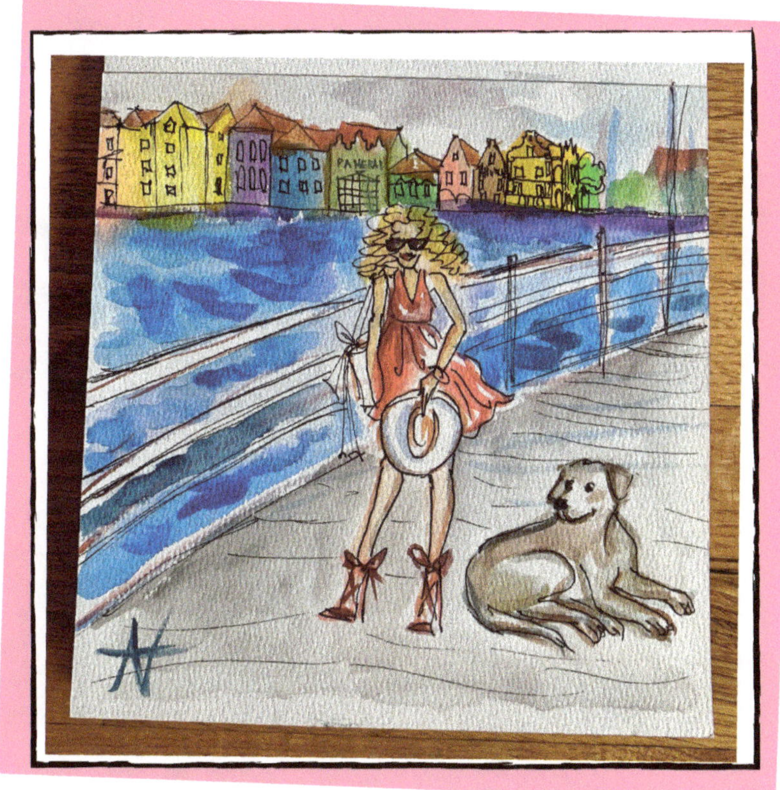

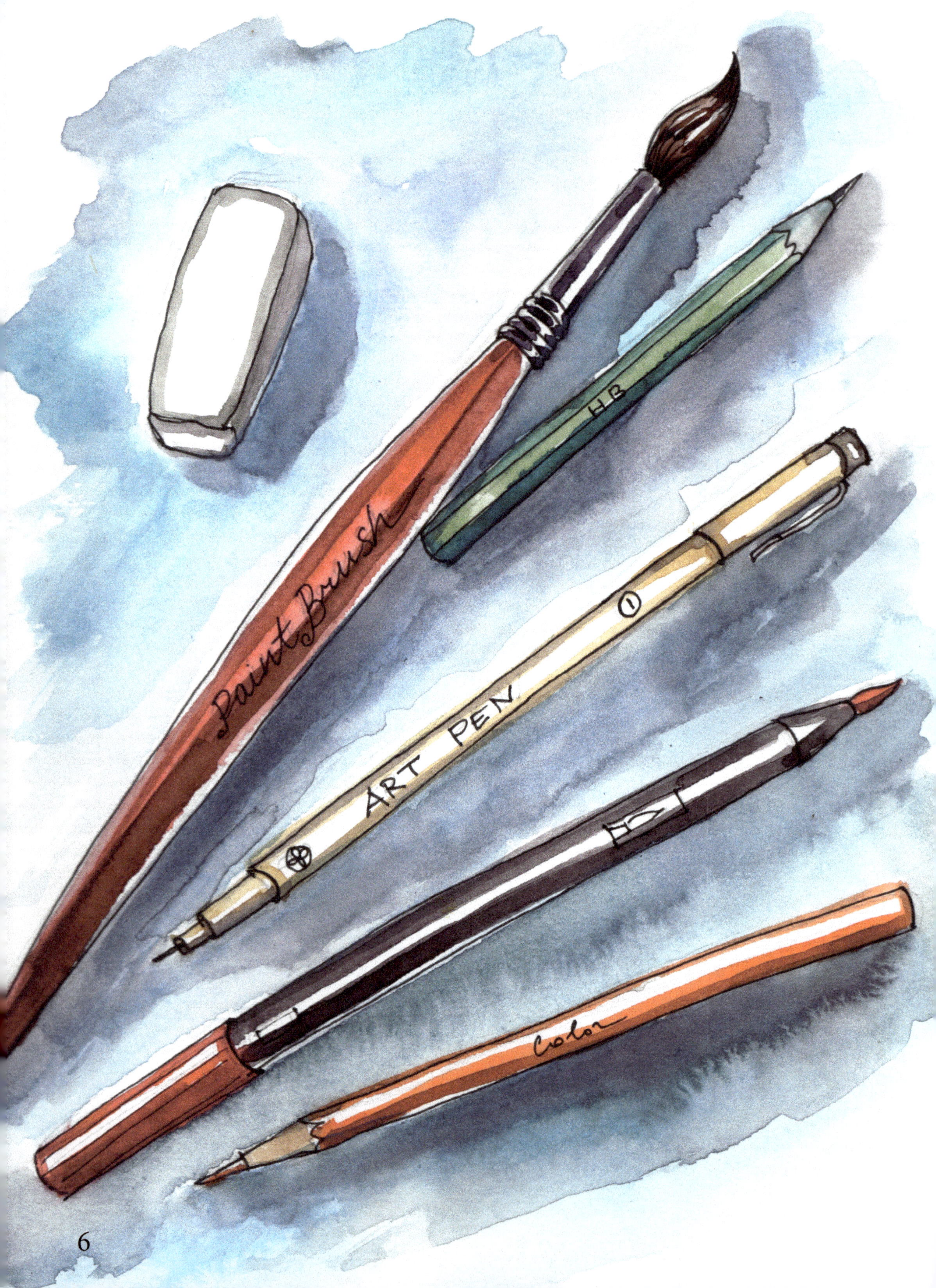

Paint Brush
HB
ART PEN
color

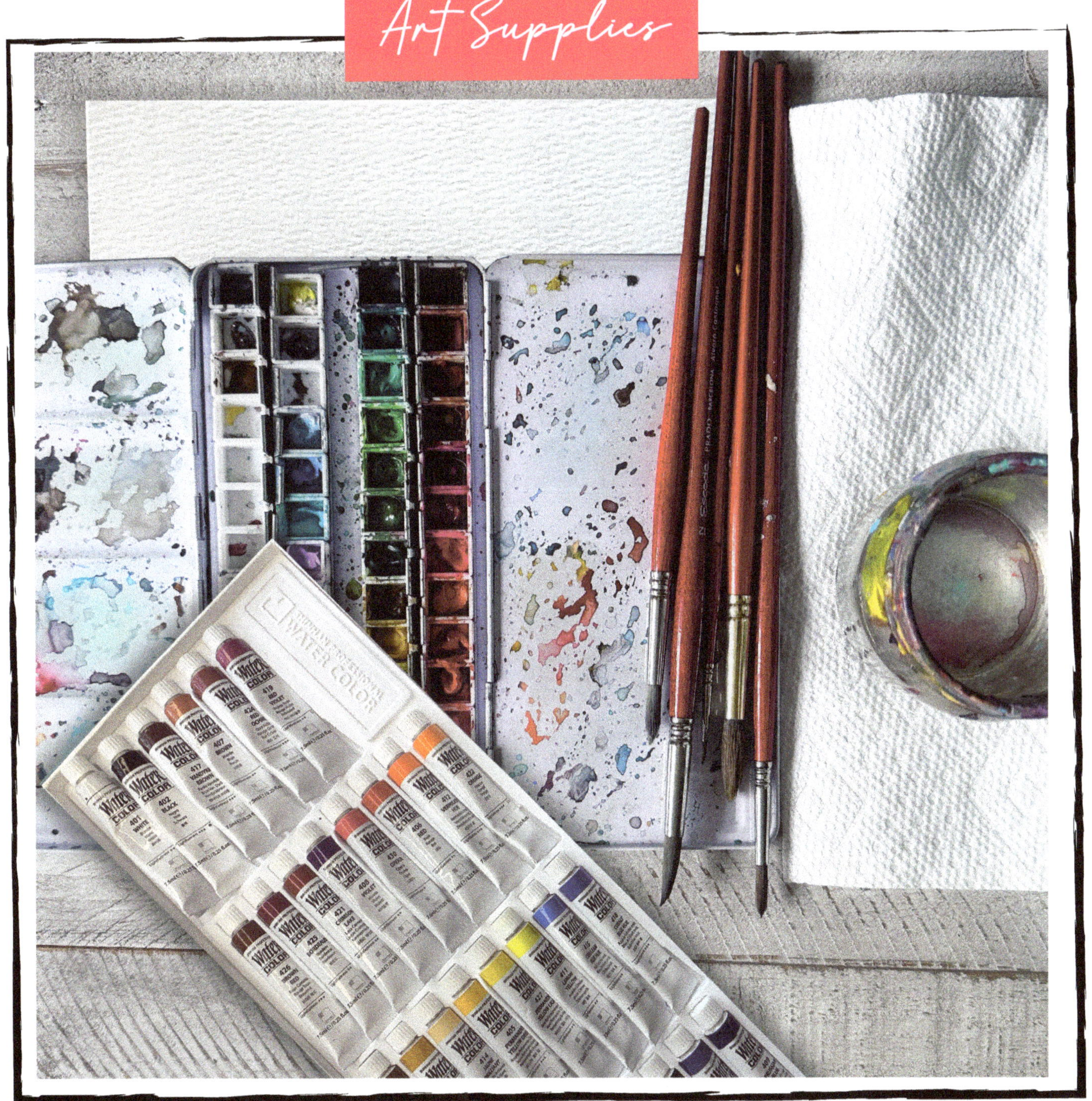

Here are the art supplies I recommend you have on hand to create your fabulous fashion scenes:

1. Set of tube watercolors
2. Watercolor tin pallet
3. Set of round synthetic watercolor brushes
4. Watercolor paper 140 lb
5. Paper towels
6. Jar of water

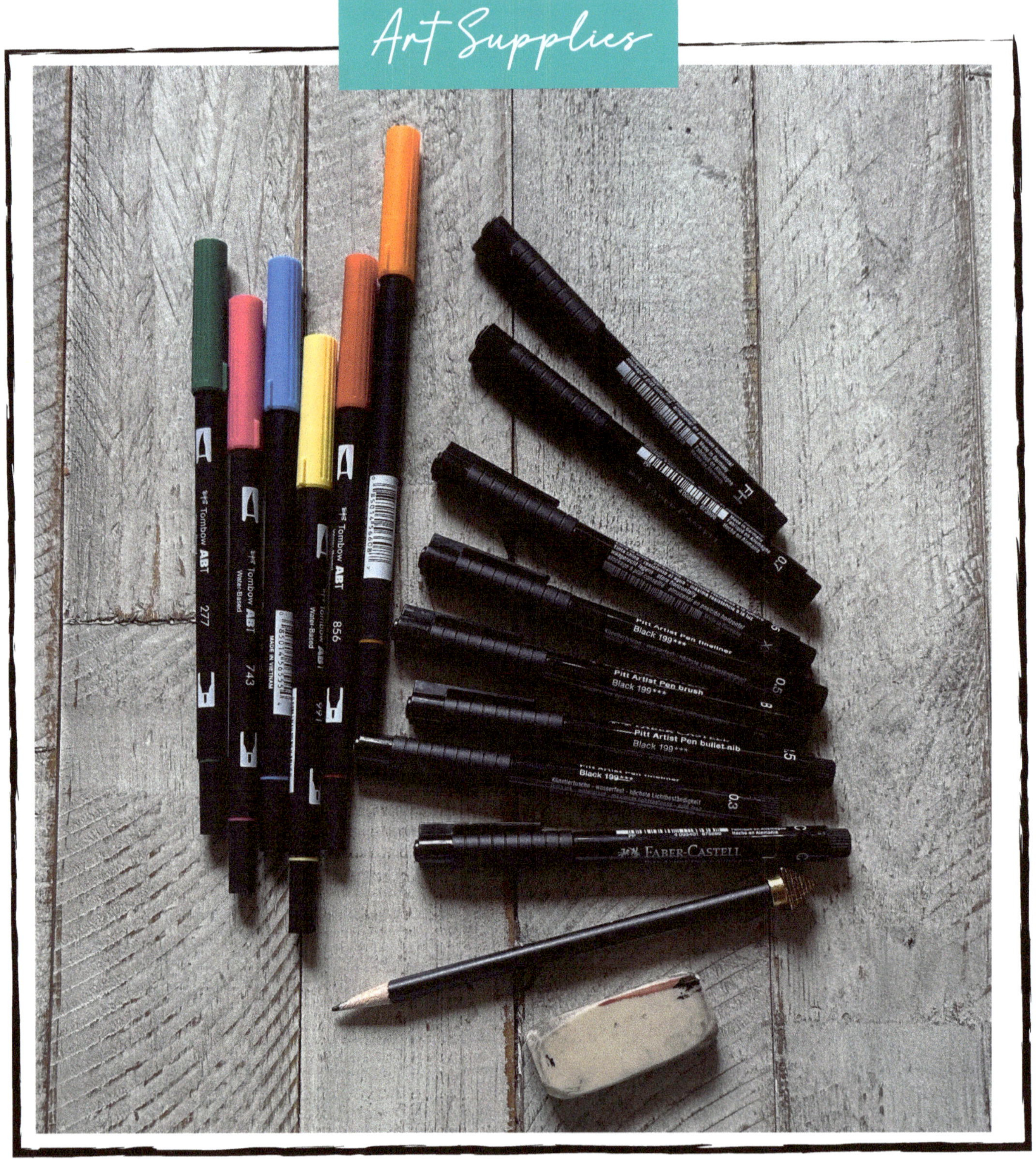

In addition to watercolors, you will also need:

1. HB Pencils
2. Erasers
3. Set of artist pens of various thicknesses
4. Set of brush marekers

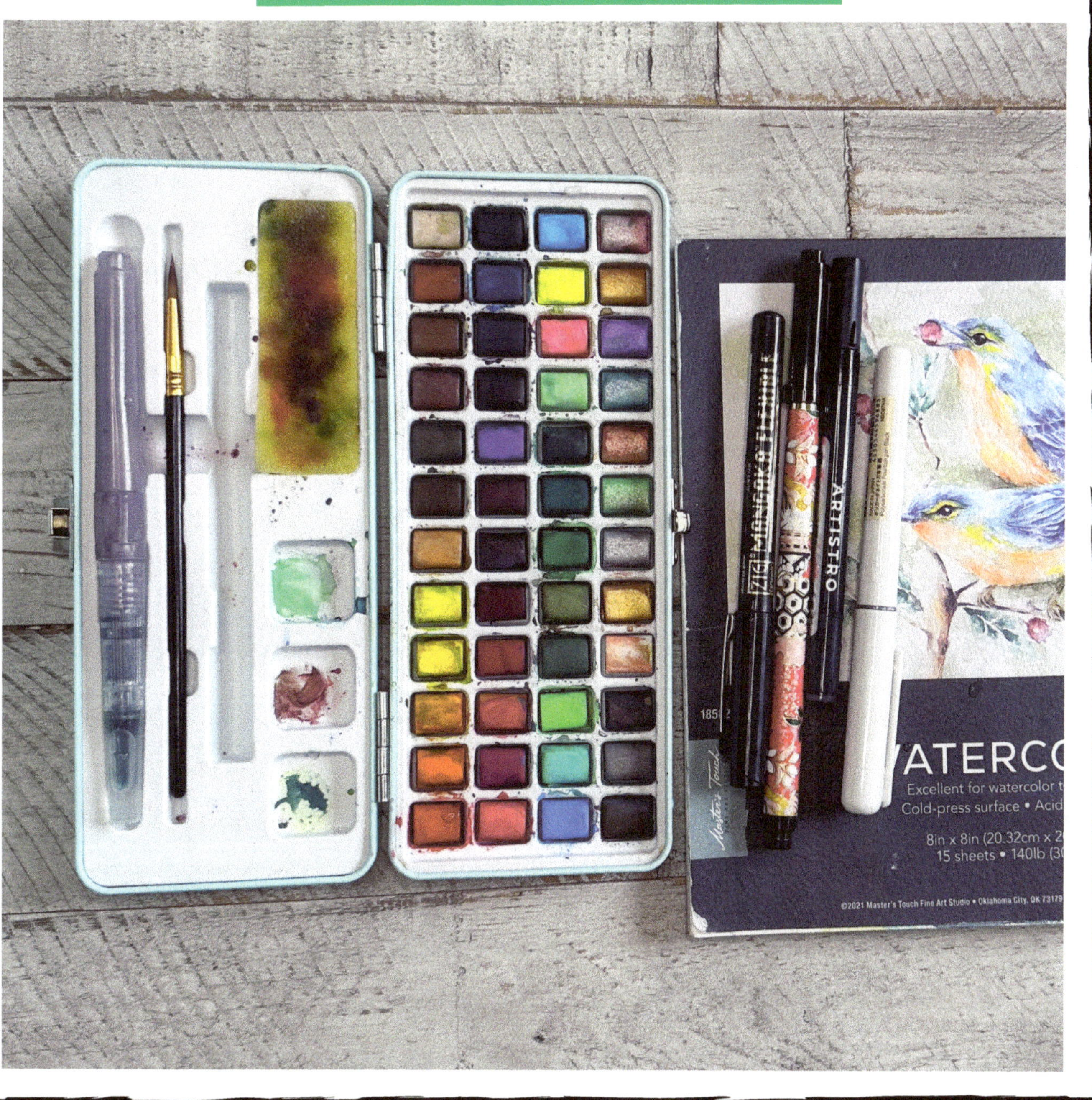

If you decide you want to try drawing and painting on location, I highly recommend you get a travel watercolor set. As well as a small watercolor pad that is more portable. You can also bring along some pens. The tiny watercolor travel set usually comes with a brush pen that you can fill with water, a sponge for wiping off colors, plus optional supplies like simple pens or brushes. Travel sets are a super convenient way to do your live art on location.

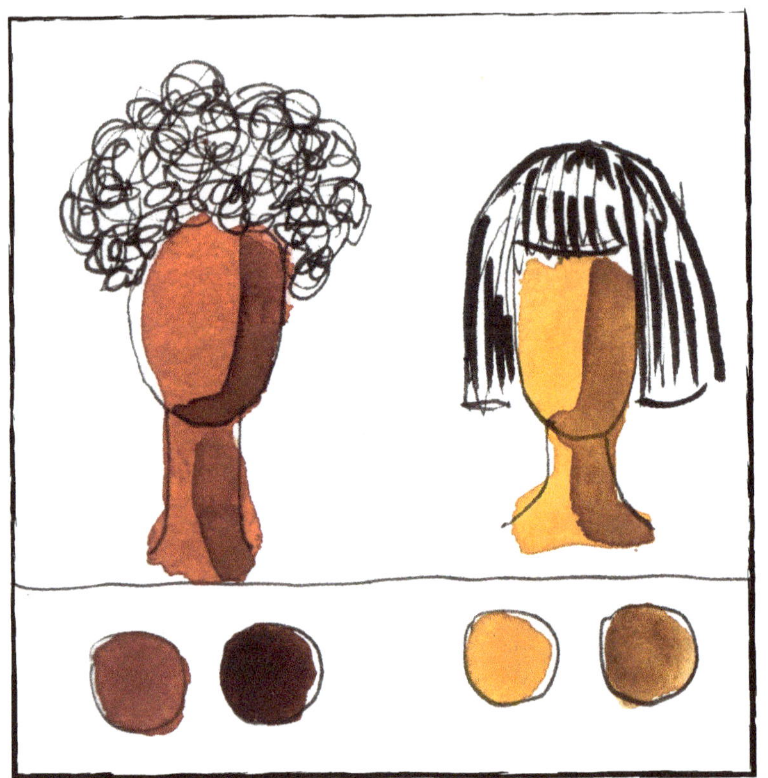

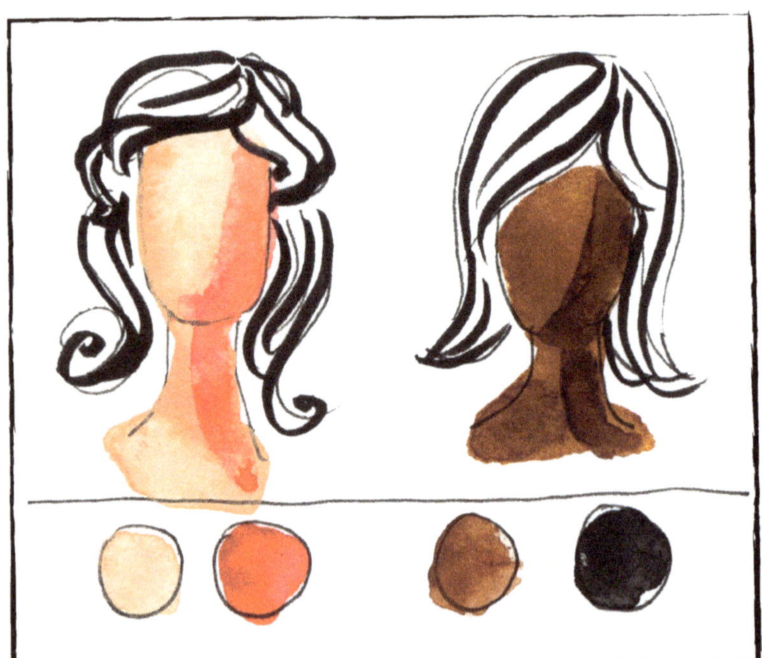

Fashion illustrators do not shy away from color.

While there are ways to work in muted colors or black and white, fashion illustration is often associated with bright, vibrant, juicy colors.

Many color tube sets come with every color you will possibly need for your fashion art, with and without having to mix the colors.

Sets come in various shades and tones of blues, yellows, reds, greens, browns, violets and their cousins.

You can mix colors to create shading, and you can also use the available darker shades that come in the tubes. The color names vary, therefore I will not list them here. However, you can always approximately match the colors you have to the ones you see in this book.

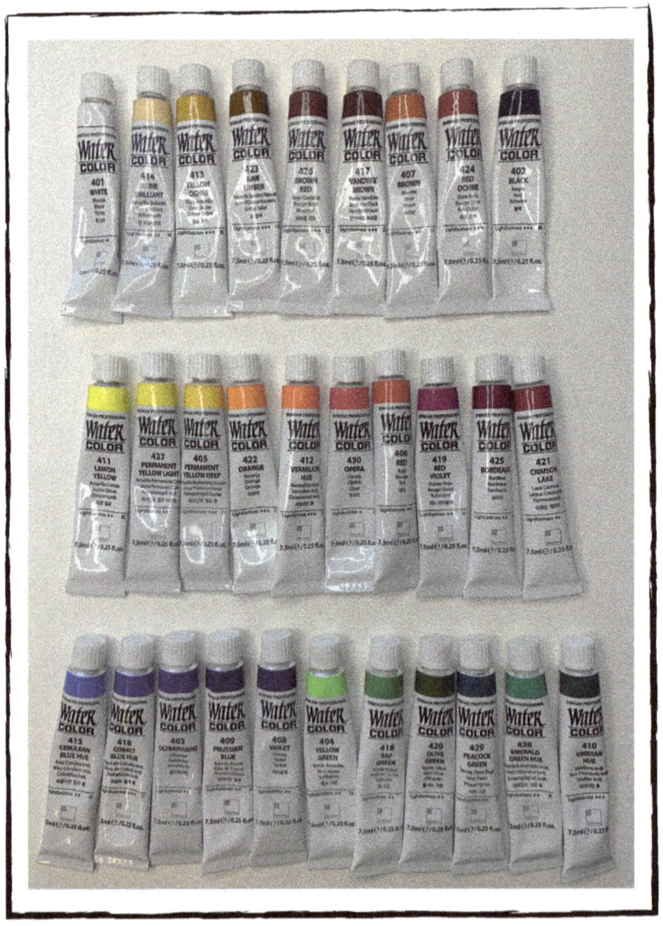

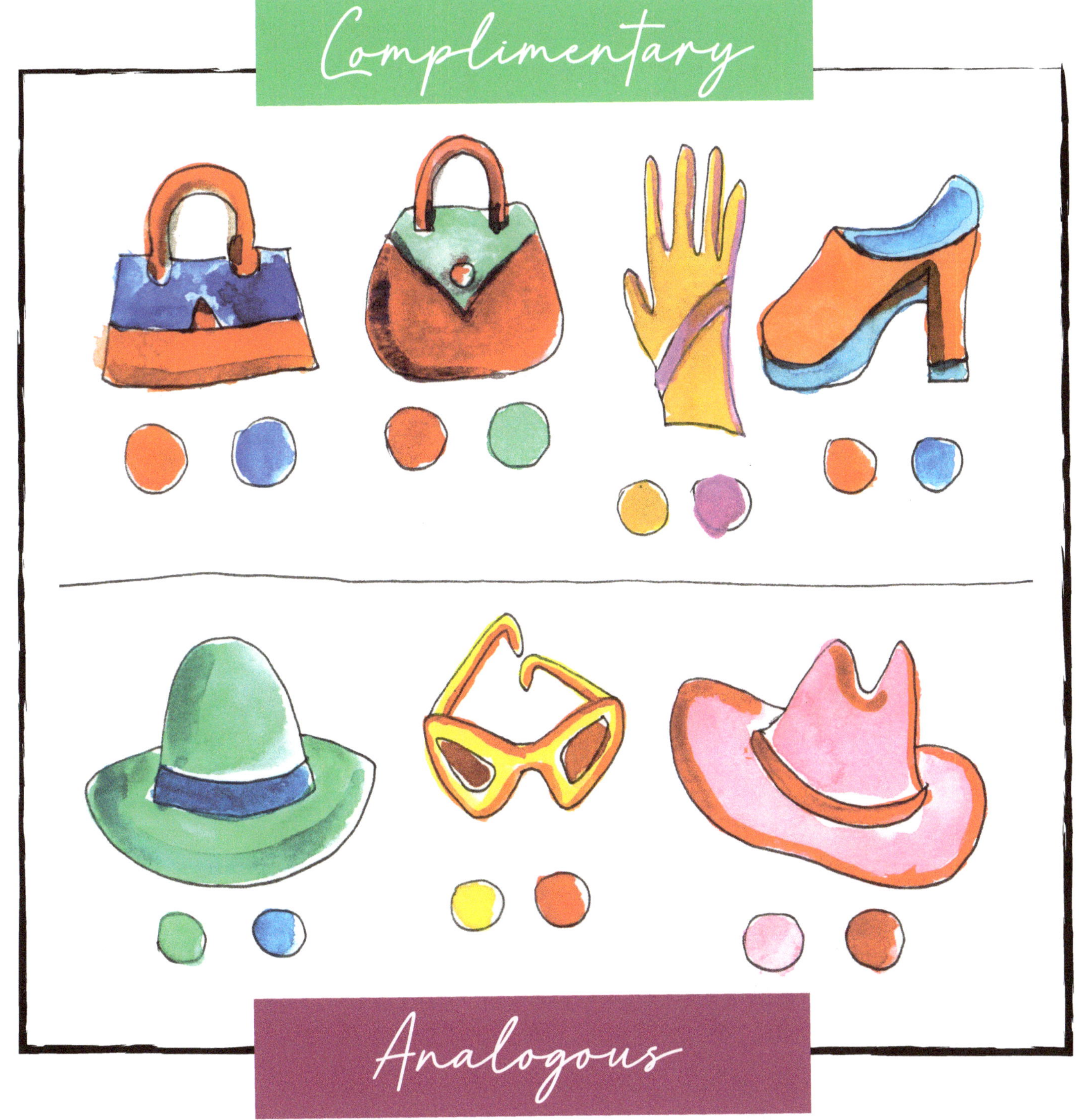

When illustrating fashion, you can use complimentary colors and/or analogous colors. For example, complimentary colors are: red and green, blue and orange, yellow and violet. Analagous colors, are colors from the same family, or ones that are near each other. For example, pink and red, blue and green, yellow and orange. Both options can look quite interesting when we illustrate them. Avoid things from getting muddy when you paint. Wait for your first layer to dry before applying shading, and don't over-mix colors. Keep it simple.

Fashion Figure Basics

This is a review of what we learned about the fashion figure in the previous book "Fashion Illustration Techniques in Watercolor."

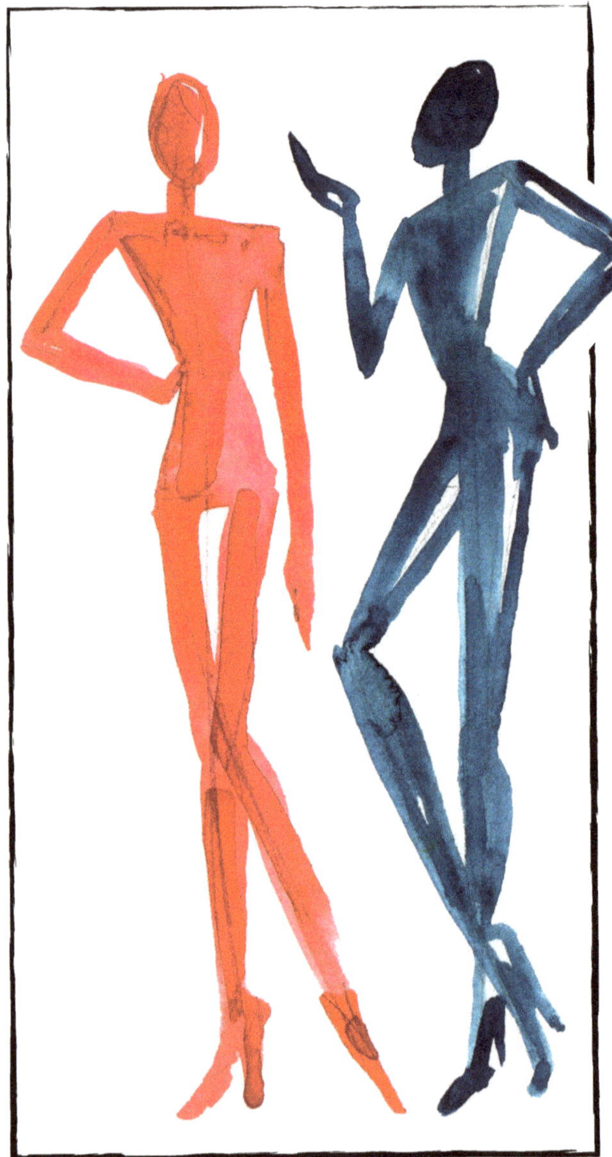

Poses

Keep them dynamic. Tilt hips and shoulders in opposite directions, or make one of the legs bent or kicked to the side.

Balancing

When you draw, imagine a straight line going from the center of the neck bone to the supporting leg, or the leg our figure stands on.

Proportions

When you create your fashion figure sketches, always leave plenty of room for legs. Shoot for 1/3 or less of your body being the distance from the top of the head to the hips, and the other 2/3 legs from hips to toes. Thus, make the head small and have it start close to the top of your paper.

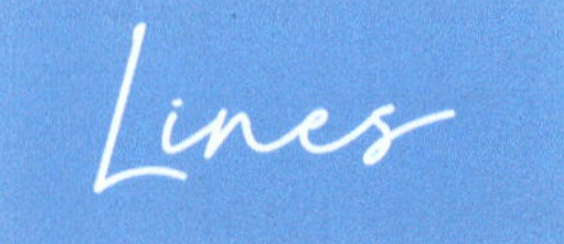

Lines

Make your drawings with strong and expressive lines. Do not overwork your drawing. Fashion drawings are supposed to look spontaneous and fresh, even a little sloppy (in a good way.)

Even in exaggerated figures, we must adhere to basic anatomical rules, that, if not followed, can make our drawings look amateur and childish.

Some of the basics include: The elbows (when arms are down) should hit at the waist. The hands (when arms are down) should hit at mid/thigh. One of the common mistakes is making the arms way too short. The eyes should be placed at about mid line of the head. When we draw hair, we draw it in strands, the way it would naturally grow for straight or wavy hair. For super curly or textured hair, we create a pattern or a texture and curved outline of the hair. For some examples, see drawings inside this book.

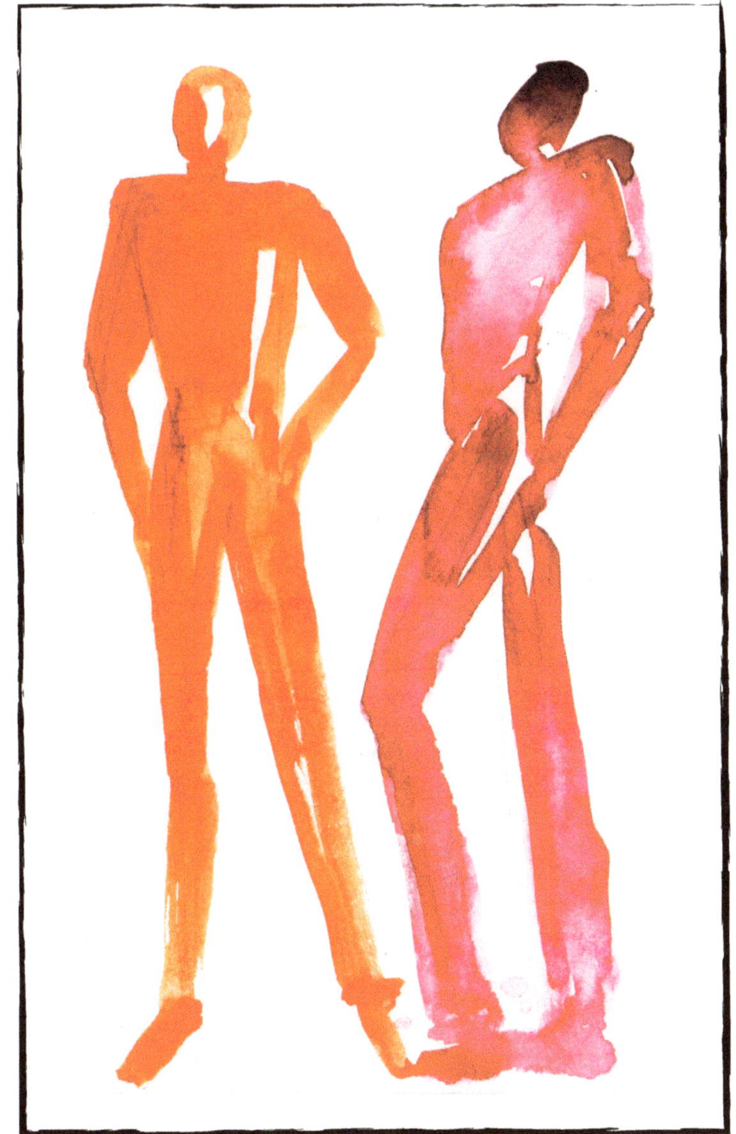

Differences

Also keep in mind slight differences when you draw male vs female fashion figures. Men have broader shoulders and narrower hips. Their torso is longer and their legs would be shorter. As well, their poses would be a bit less expressive or less dynamic than those of women. While still having a fashion flare. For example, a man can have his hand in jacket or pants pocket or have one of his legs slightly bent.

Making Your Mark

watercolor, markers, pens

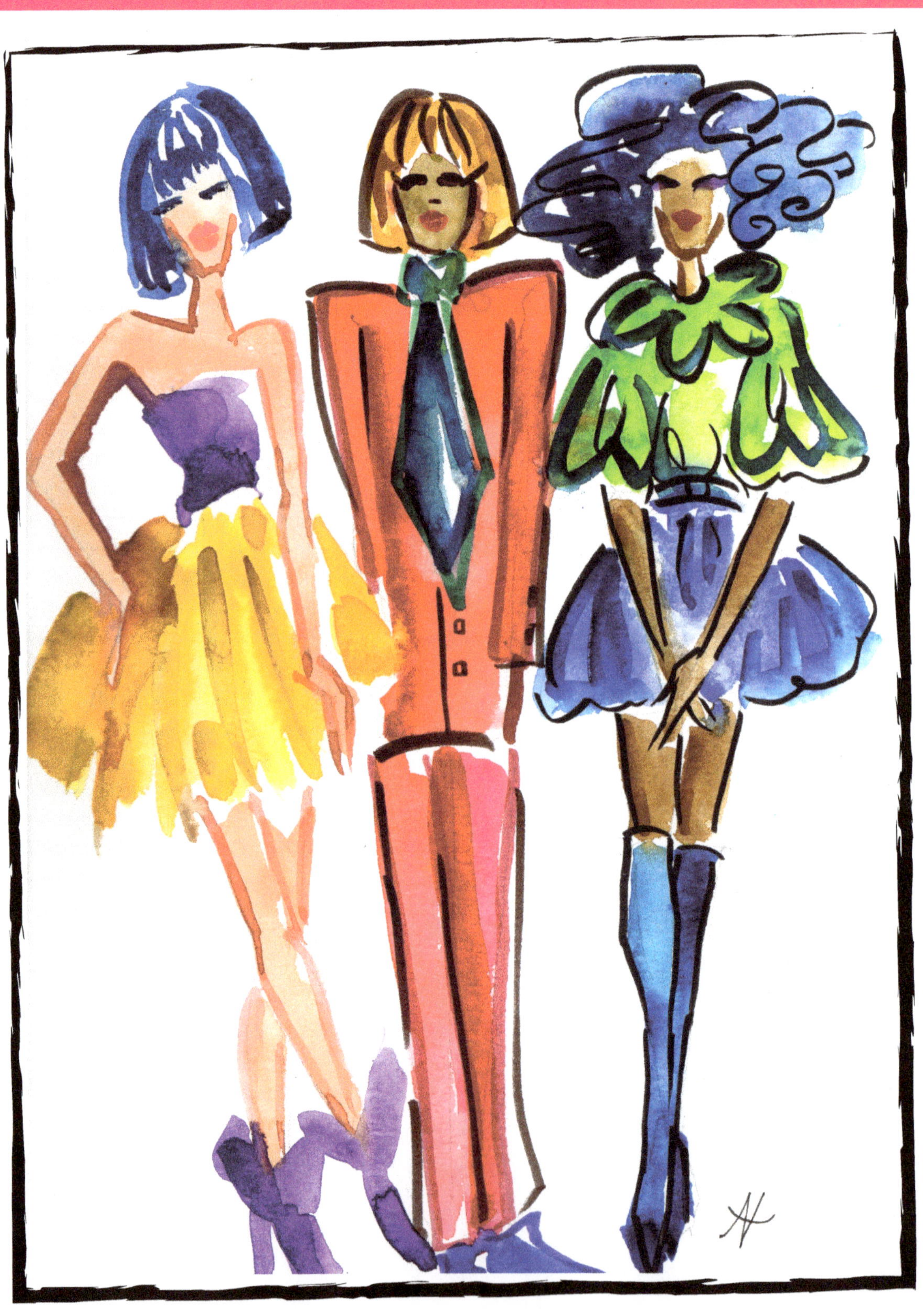

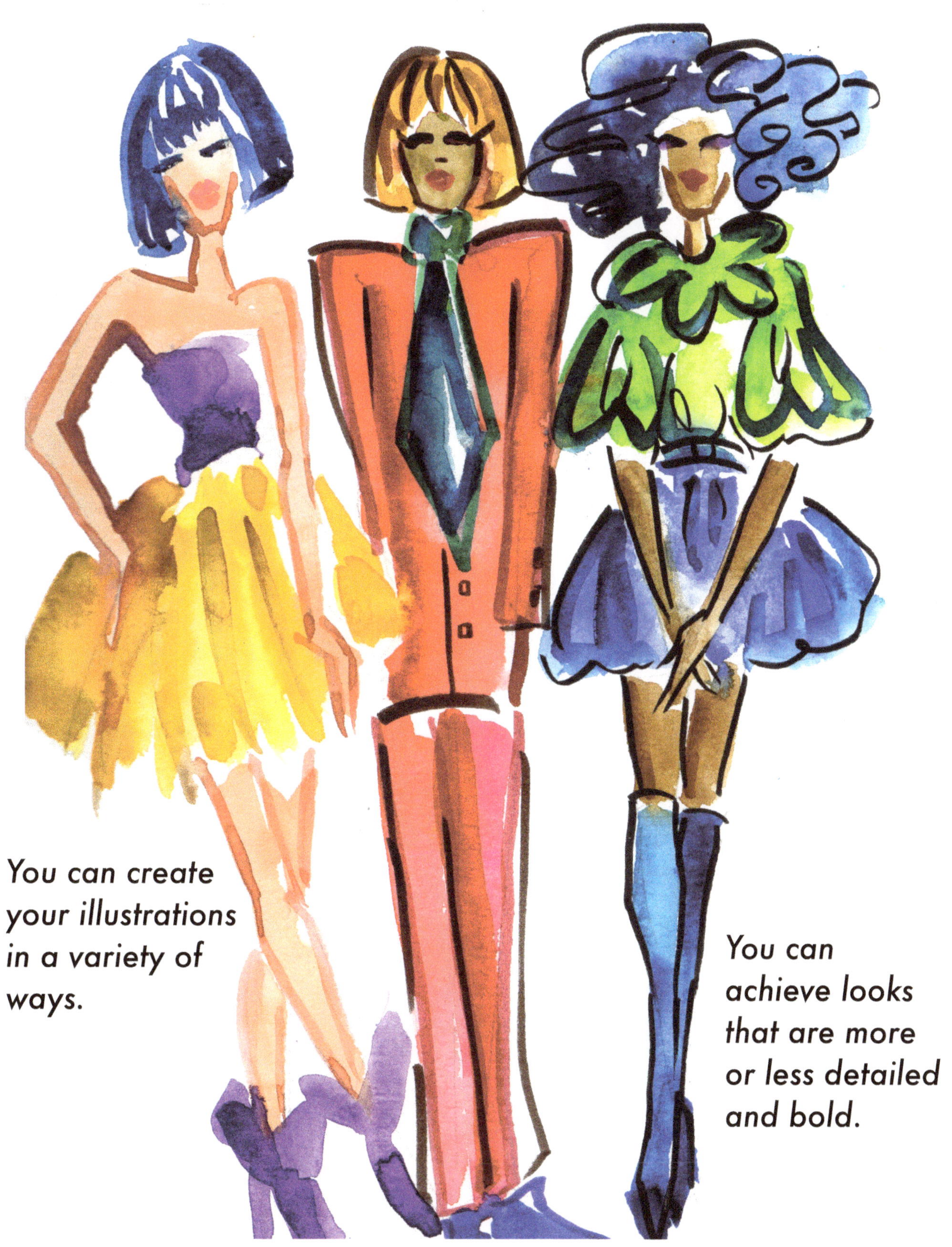

You can create
your illustrations
in a variety of
ways.

You can
achieve looks
that are more
or less detailed
and bold.

Lady in yellow was painted in watercolor only. Lady in red was painted and then outlined in parts with color brush markers. Blue lady was painted in watercolor and then outlined in parts with a black brush pen.

A Fashion Figure in a Scene

When we consider drawing and painting a fashion figure in a scene, we have to think about creating an effective and balanced composition.

The figure is always our primary focus. Therefore, we almost always start with drawing the figure first. The figure is in the foreground. Then we can draw the background, like a fancy building or interior space.

To create an interesting contrast, you can paint the figure in watercolor, and draw the building in pen outline.

Use step by step exercises in the following pages to practice your fashion compositions.

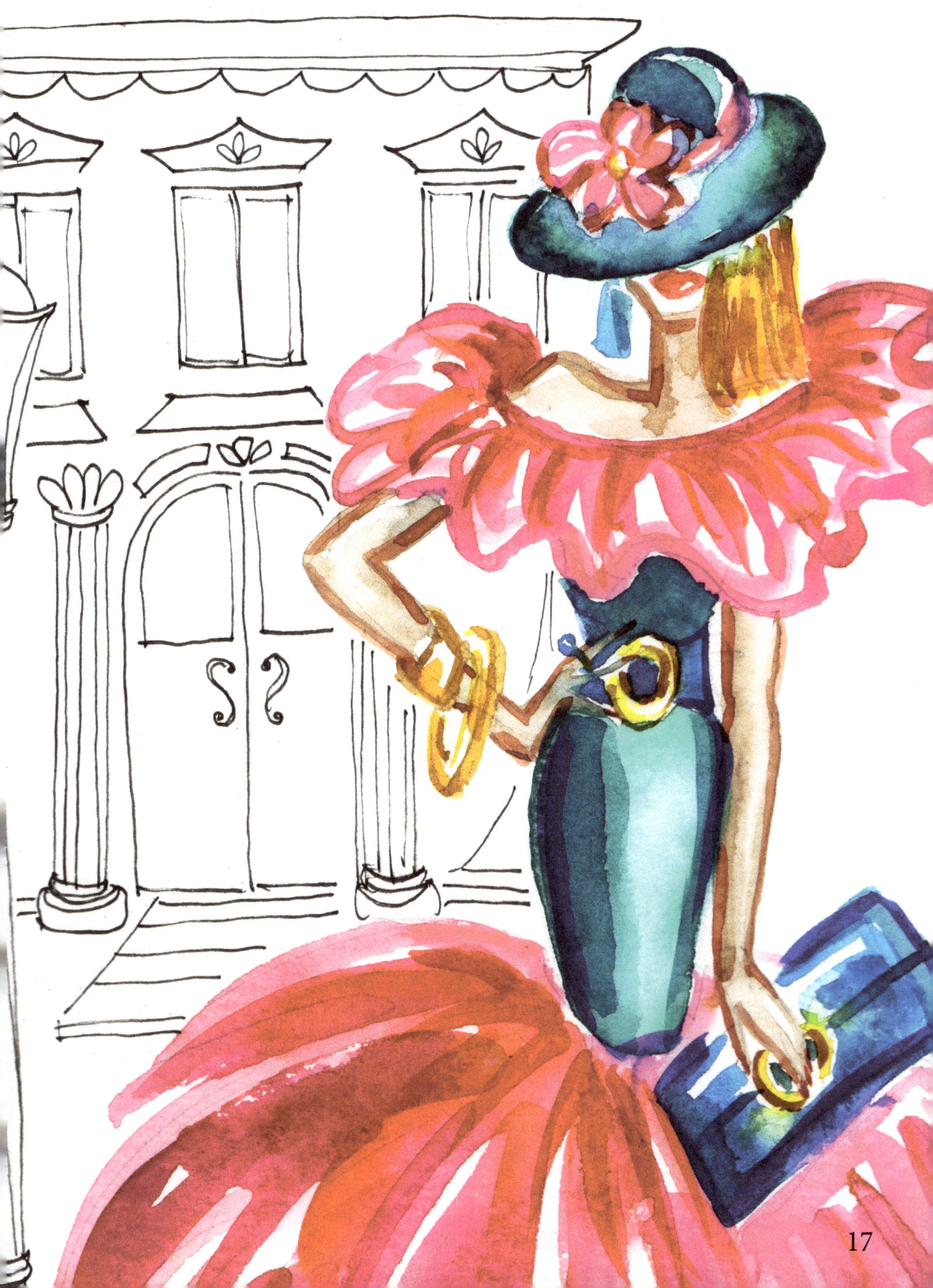

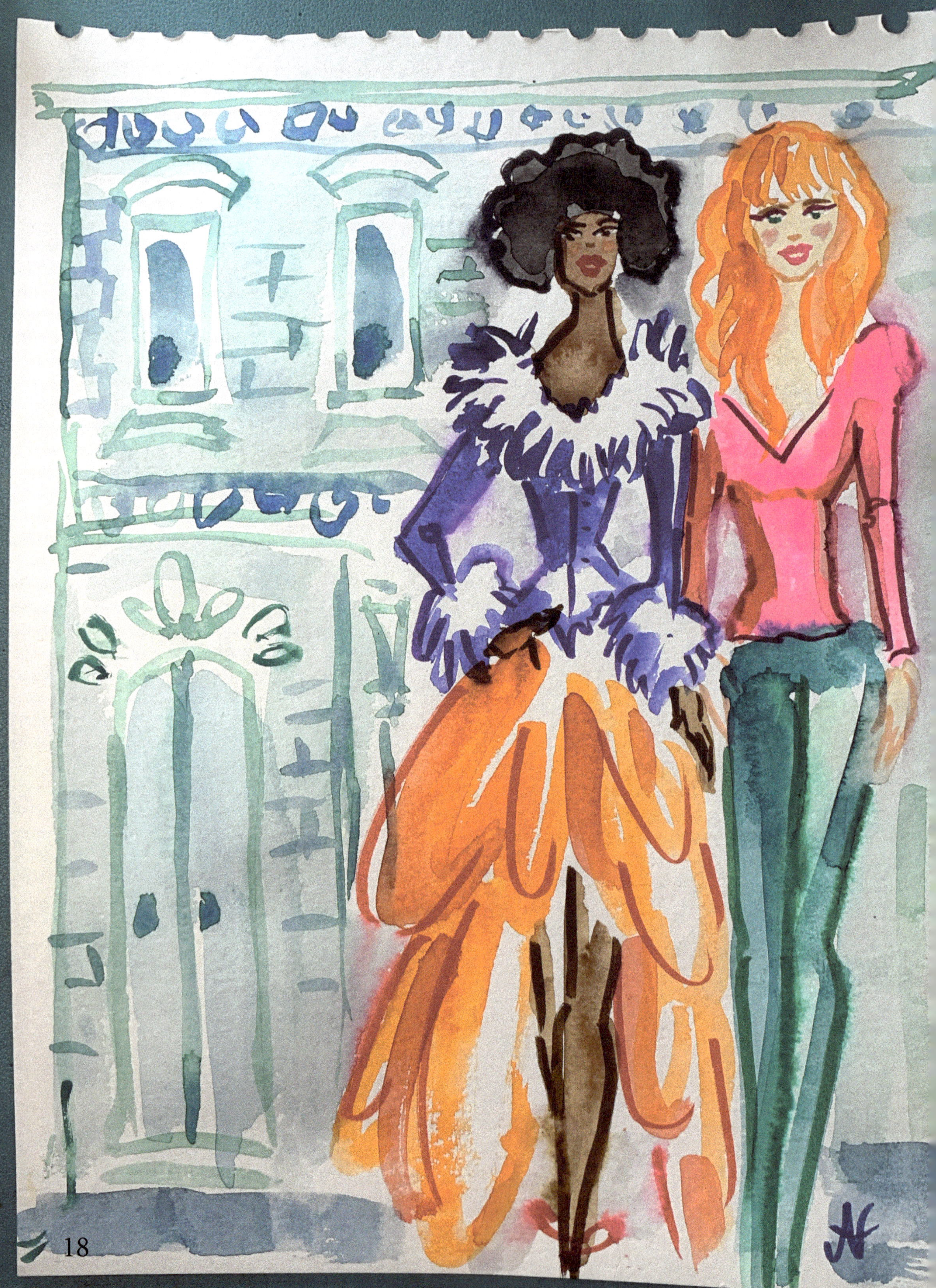

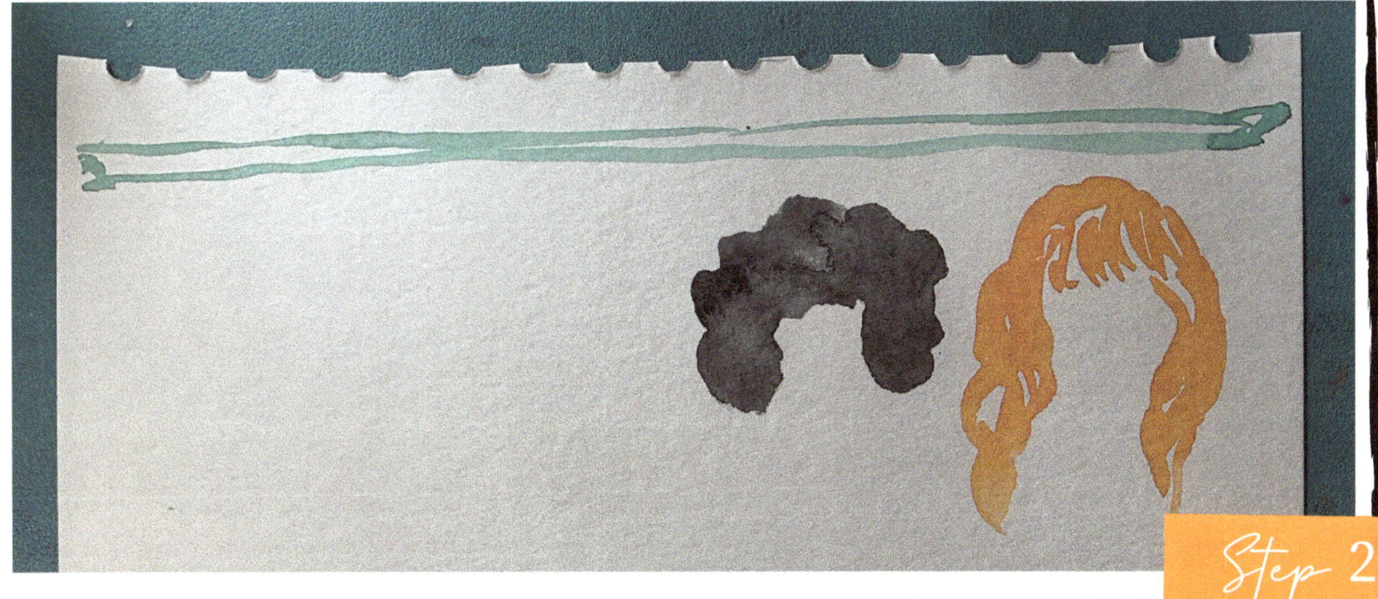

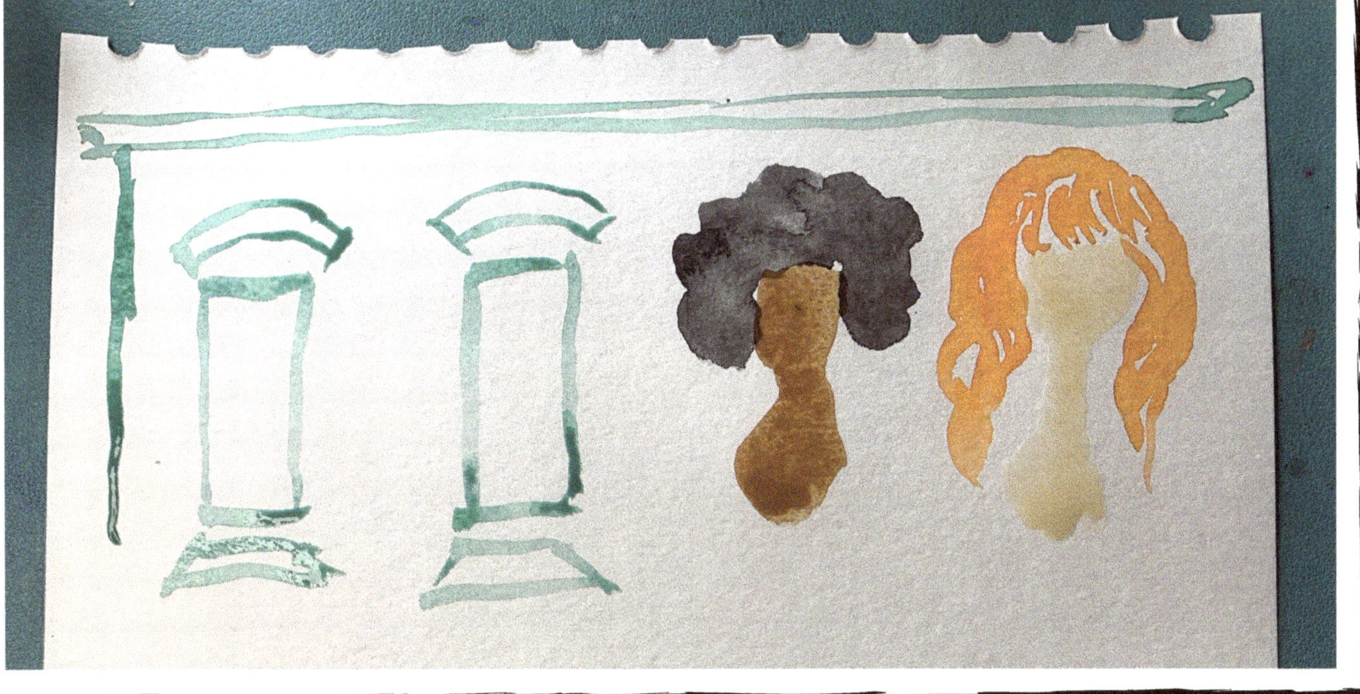

A good way to dip your feet into fashion scene illustration is to do this simple and loose watercolor exercise. Here we have two fashion figures, with a building as a backdrop. When painting in watercolor, using the white of the paper as your medium is very important. So, leave some spots white, generally where you would like to indicate the light source.

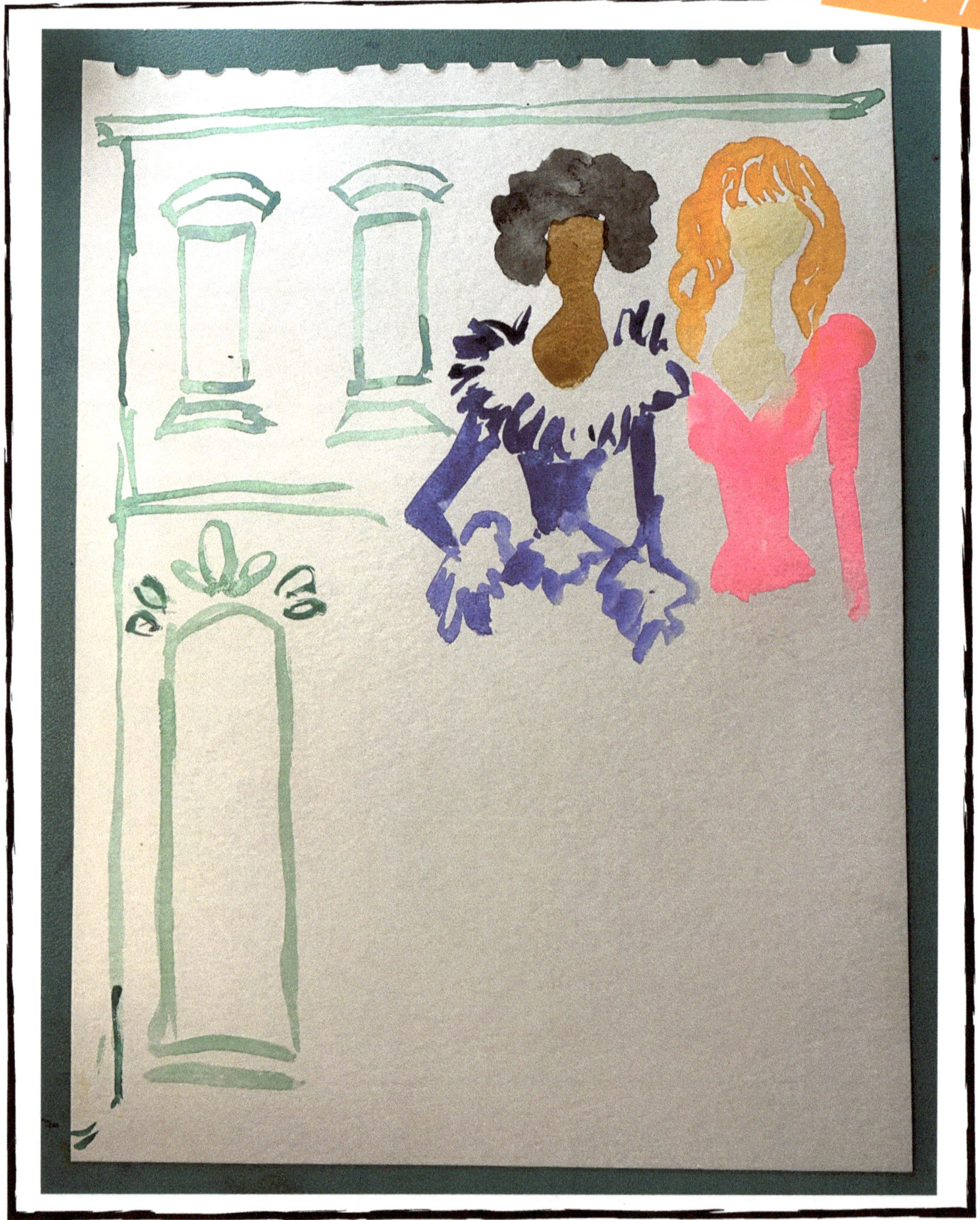

Using simple and sure strokes, paint-draw the figures' faces, hair, tops and building elements. The more sure your strokes, the more professional your illustration will look.

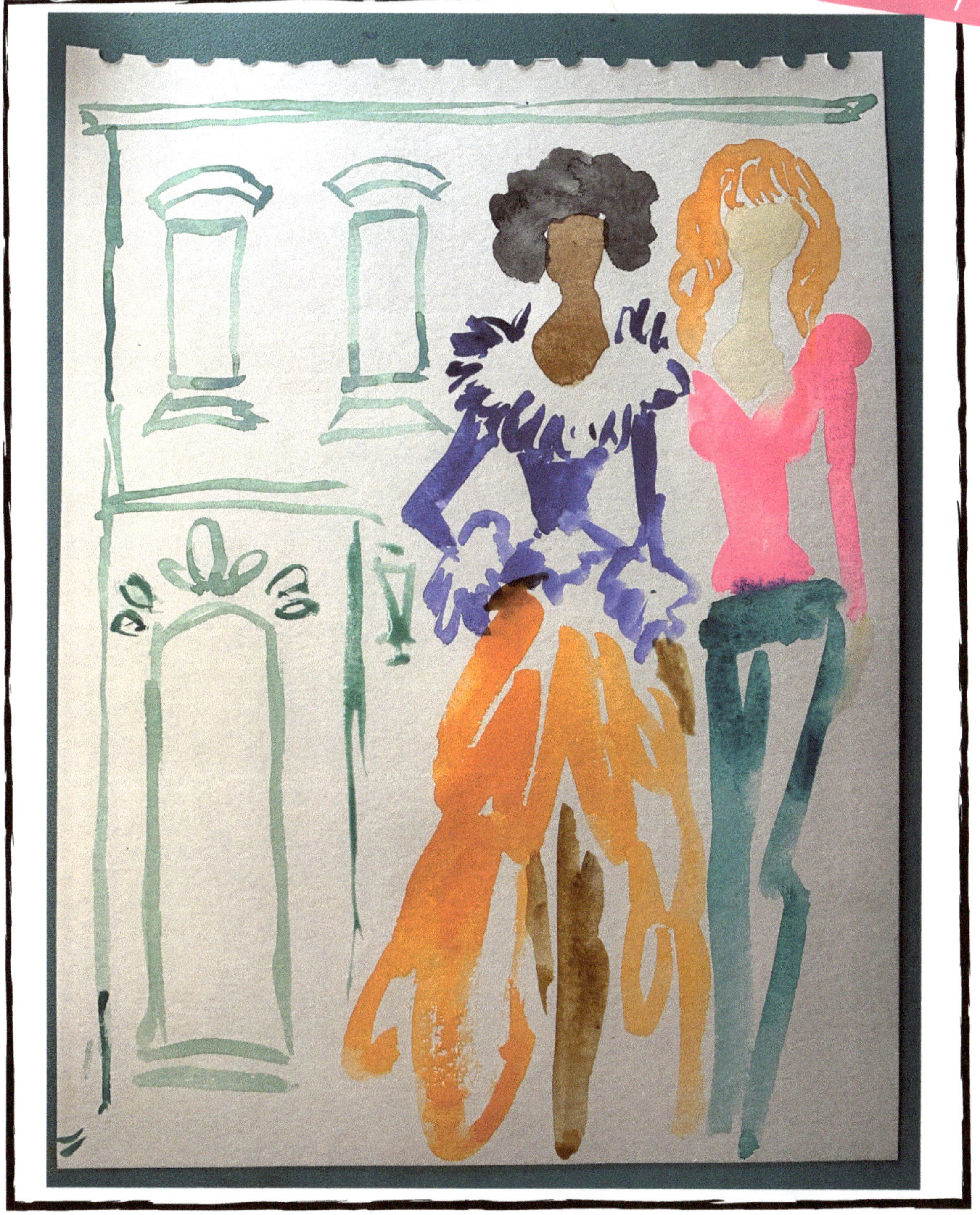

Now draw the bottom garments/legs and the rest of the elements of the building.

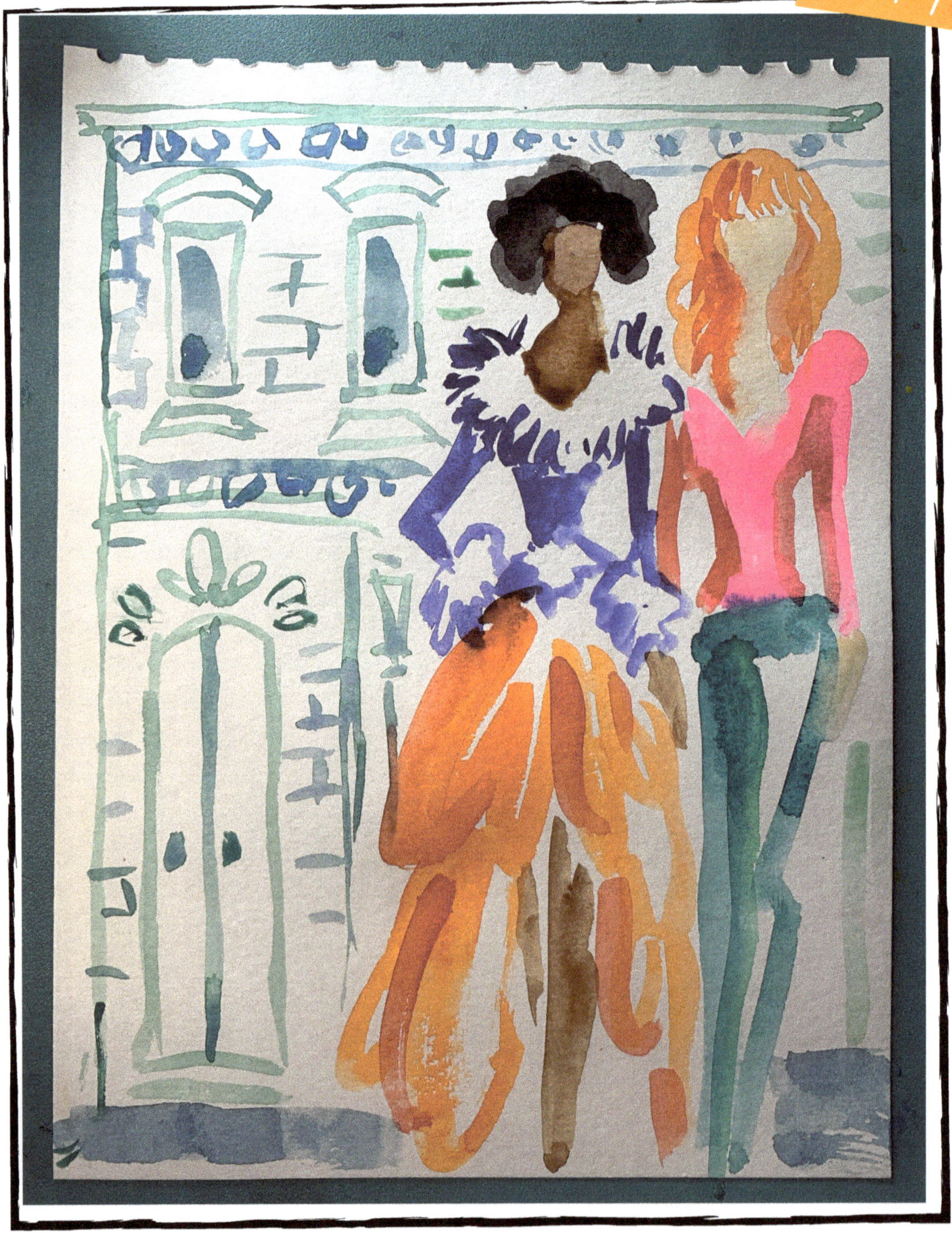

Once the first layer dries, add more details to the building and shading to the hair and the clothing.

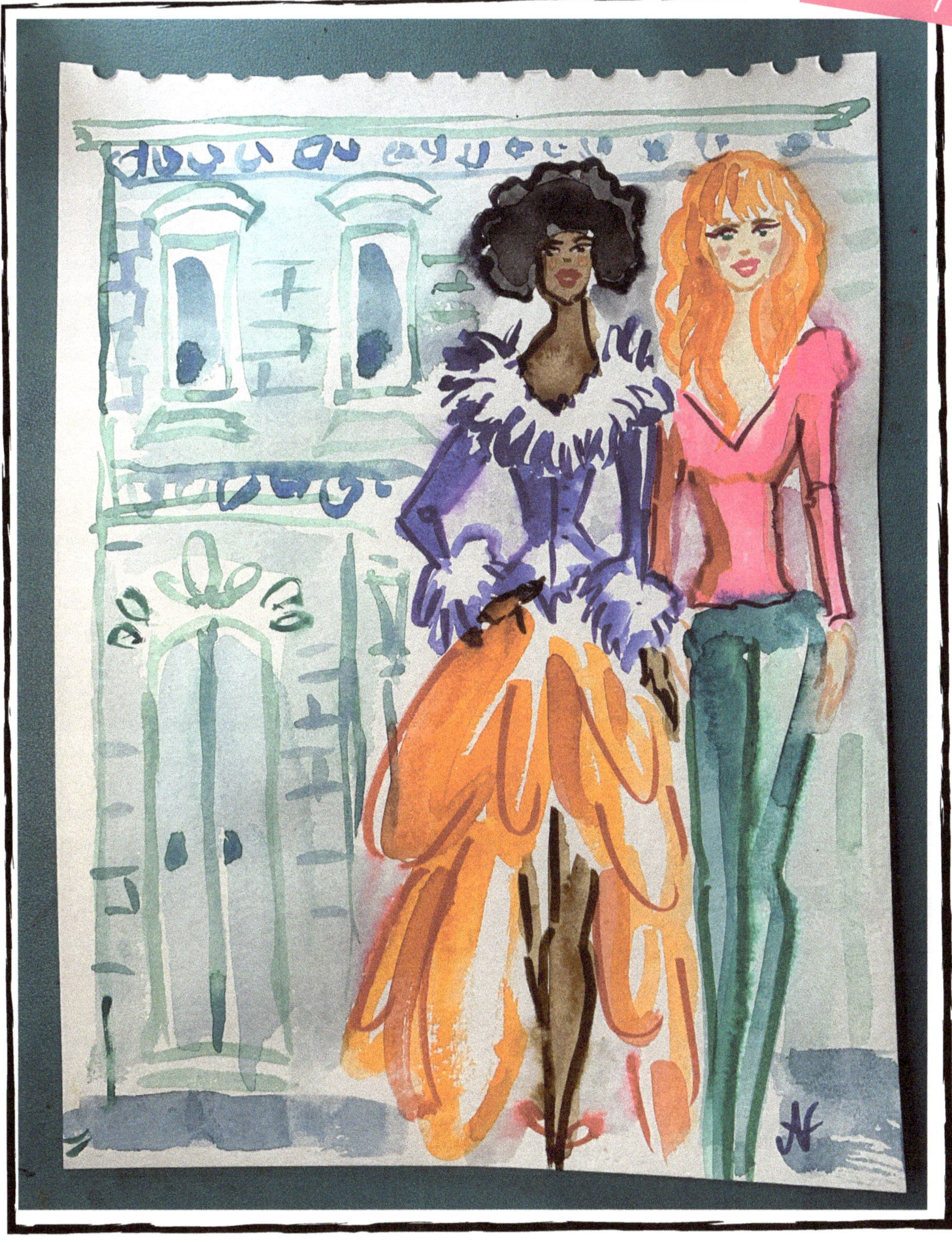

When everything dries, add faces and details on the figures with markers.

Principles of One and Two Point Perspective

When I draw, I do not first draw lines to determine the exact
and perfect points for my perspective to look accurate.
However, it is very important for an artist to know the basic
principles of perspective before they can make drawings
and paintings of scenes. Here's why.

When you understand the way perspective works, you will always
try and make your drawings look somewhat accurate. Objects
in the front will always appear larger, buildings will not appear
like they are aimlessly floating through space, but will be properly
grounded. Window and door lines will run parallel with the
perspective, rather than appearing flat. Buildings will be receding,
as they get further away, rather than awkwardly staying the same
size. You will notice the relationships of objects you depict in space,
especially as you draw from photos and life. You will understand
how your figures in the foreground, depending on their positioning,
relate to the objects in the background. For example, a far off
mountain range visually ends at a figure's shoulder, etc.

So no, you don't always need to measure out the exact vanishing
points and draw straight lines before you begin drawing each
scene, but you do need to know the basic perspective rules
and apply them to your art.

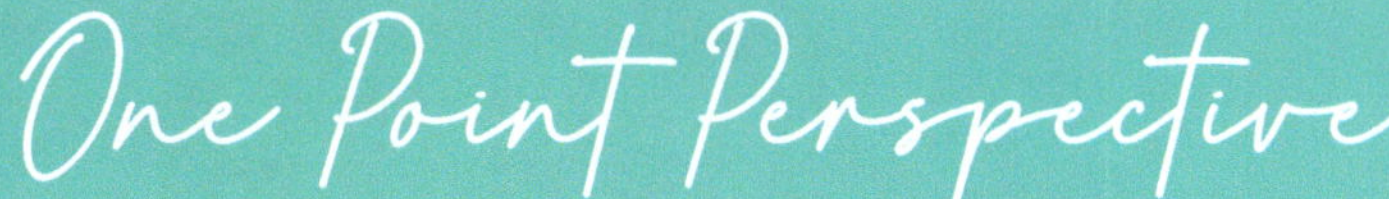

One Point Perspective

In One Point Perspective, if you draw lines from an object's corners, (here, a simple rectangle, later made into a building), the lines all converge at one singular point on the horizon line. This point is called a vanishing point. As you can see, our buildings get smaller and smaller, as they approach the vanishing point.

Two Point Perspective

In Two Point Perspective, you have two vanishing points on the horizon line.

Our corner building's sides have vanishing lines that converge at their respective vanishing points.

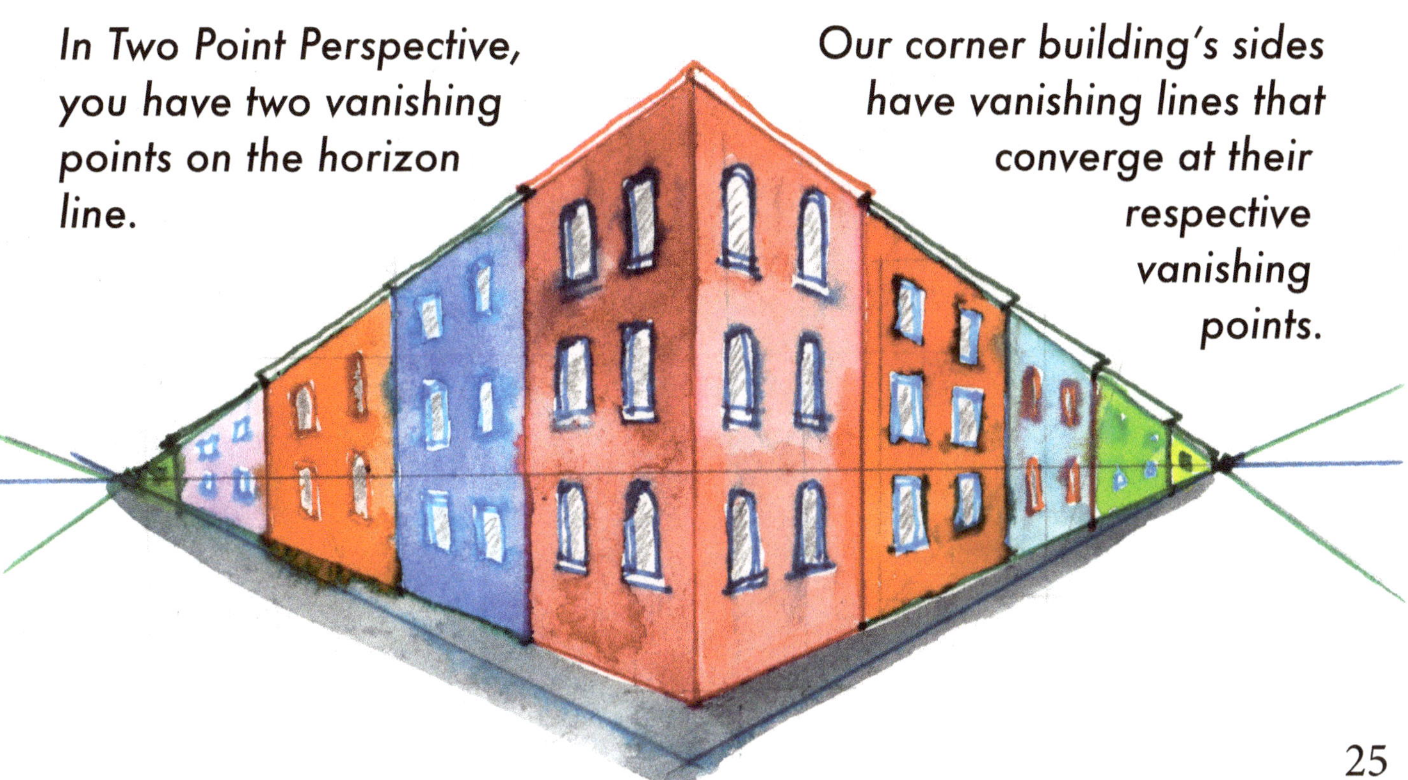

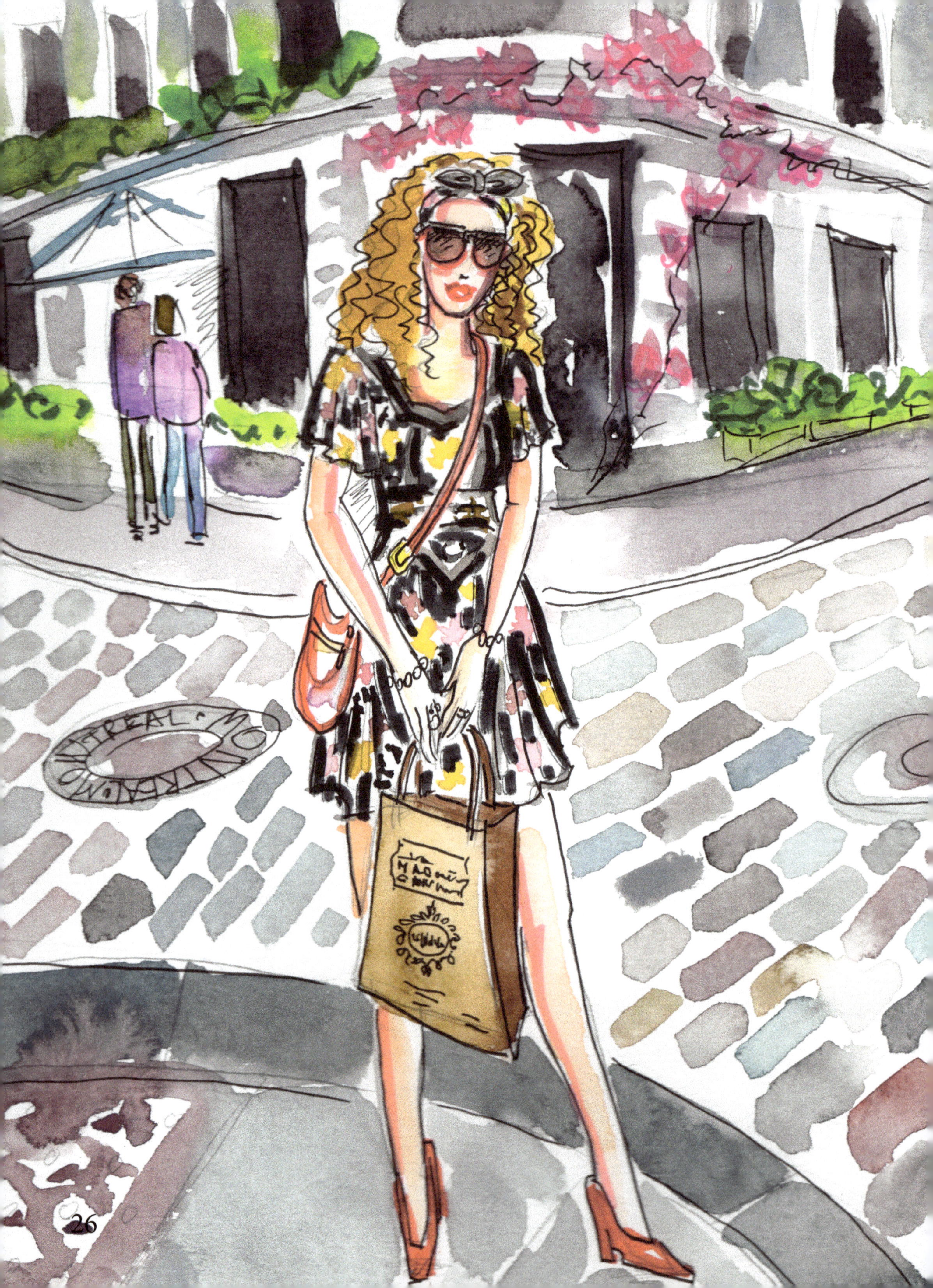

MONTRÉAL · MONTRÉAL

Painting Fashion Scenes

from photo references

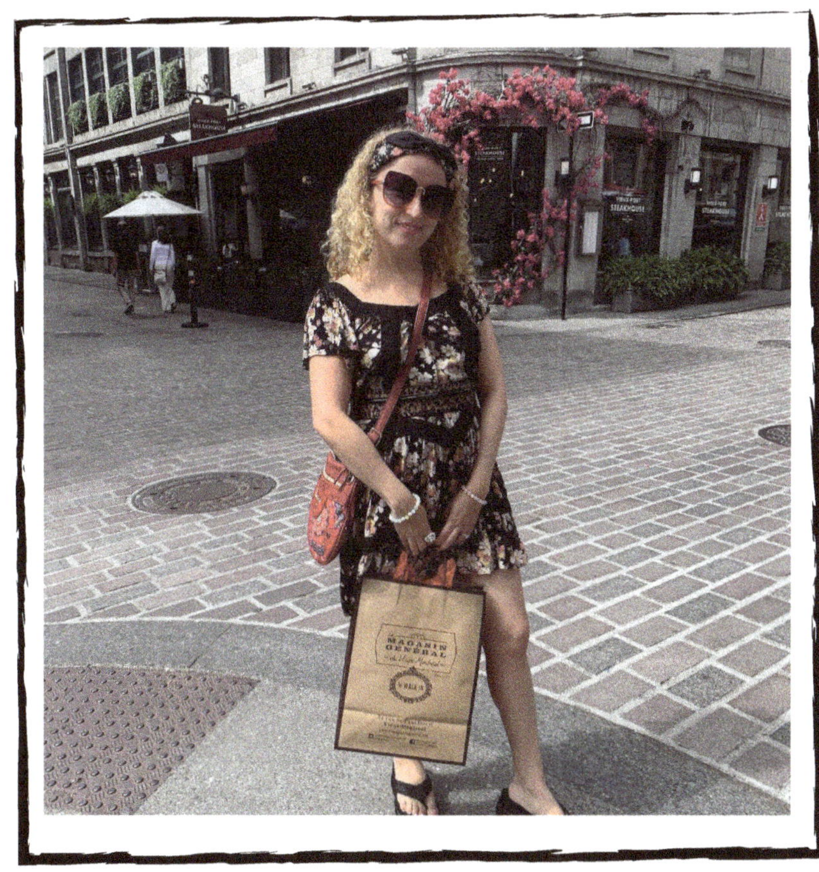

You can follow along the step by step exercises on the following pages to create your own fashion illustrations from the images in this book. After that, you can use your own photo references. Don't be afraid to go out and take pictures of cool people and places!

We will start with scenes using just one figure and a background, then we will work with two and three figures.

Backgrounds can be either cityscapes or nature, it doesn't matter. Sometimes backgrounds can include simple people silhouettes.

We always draw our main subject, the figure, first. The figure is always in the foreground, and takes up most of the page.

Picutre tips: When you decide what photo to use, pay attention to the pose, composition, interesting backgrounds. Buildings or landscapes work very well!

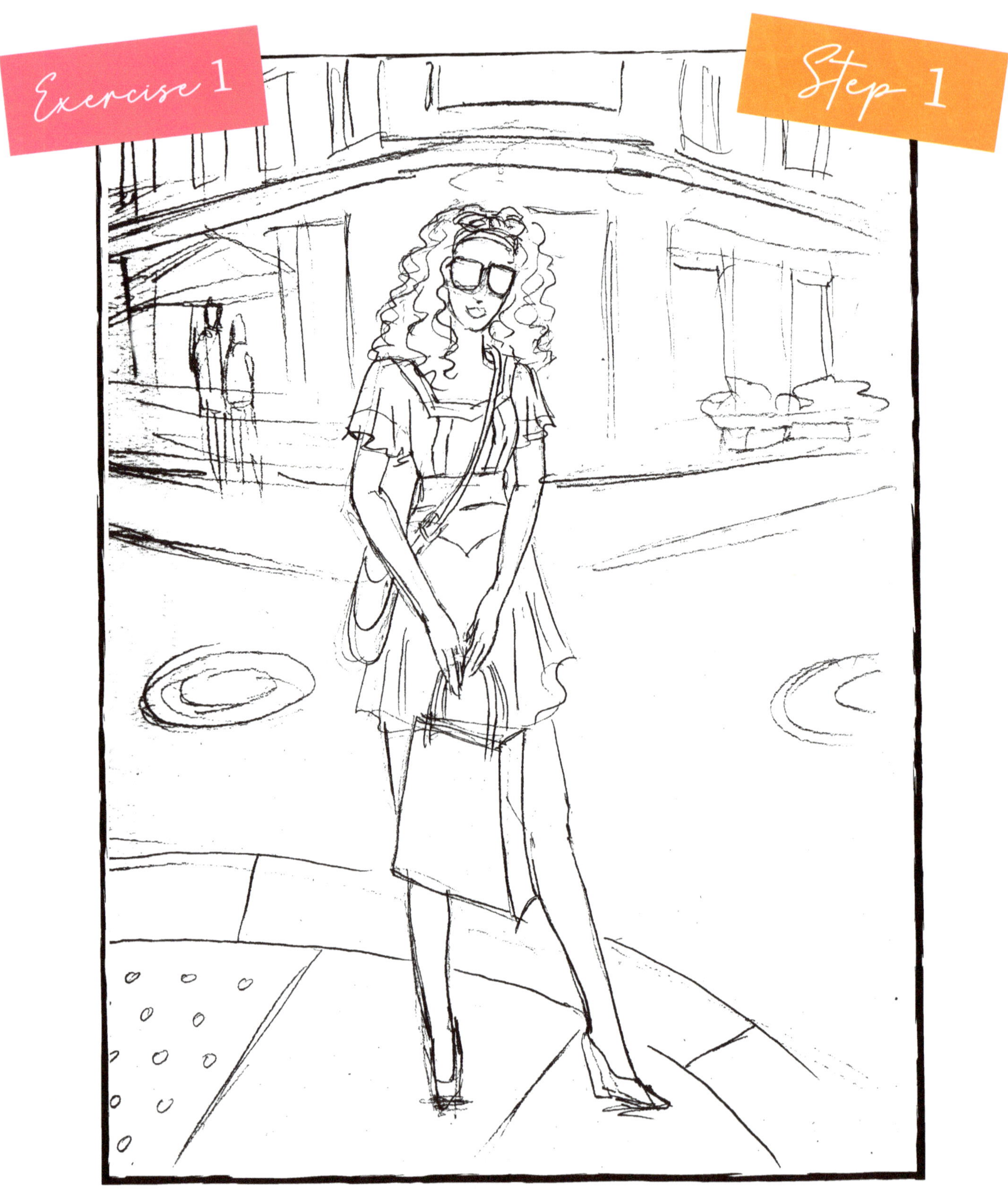

This background is a perfect example of a two point perspective. Start by sketching the figure, as our central focus. Then sketch out the interesting street backdrop.

28

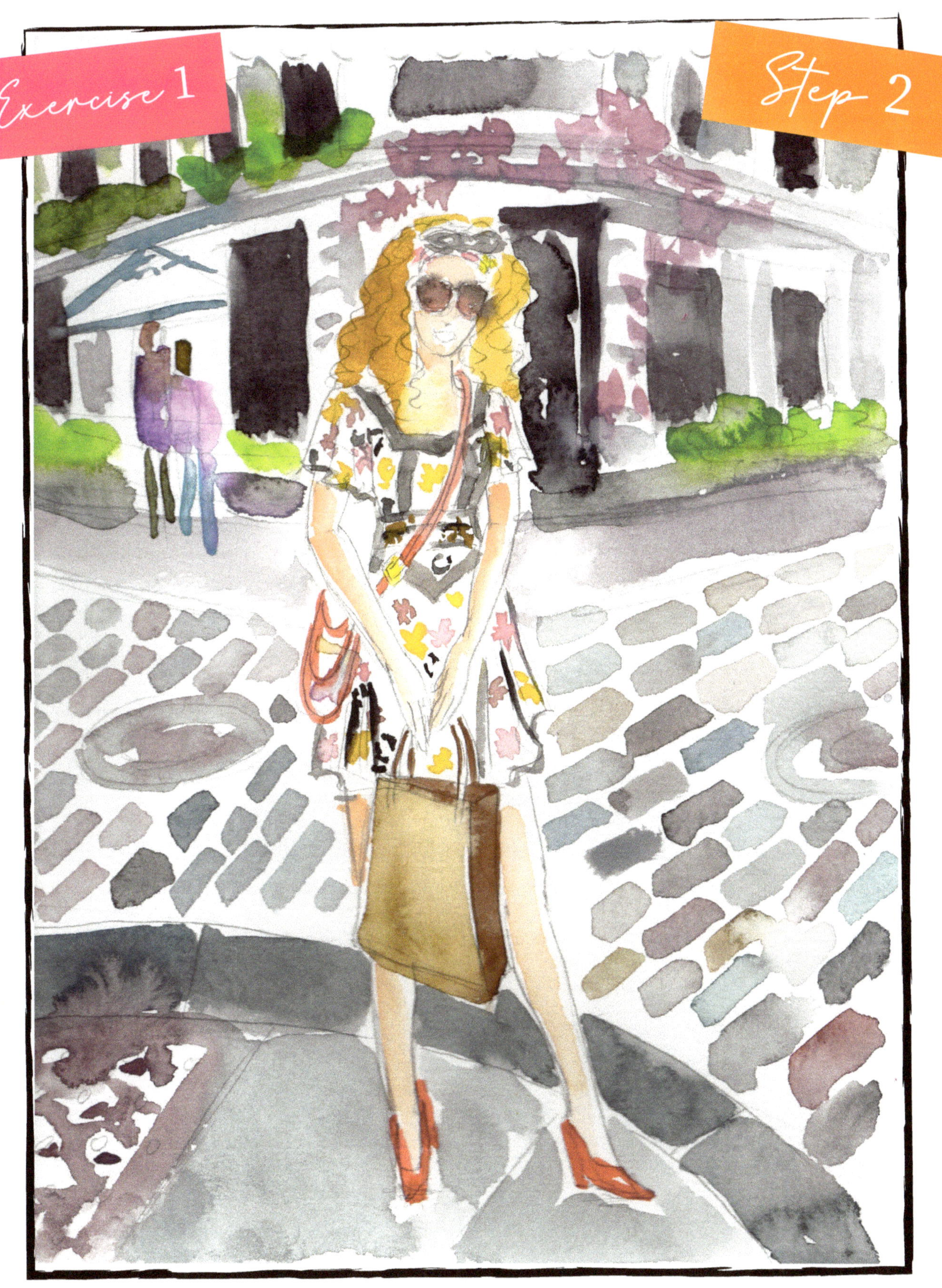

Now use light washes of watercolor for your base layer.
Let interesting bleeds happen and dab off excess water
where you do not wish it to run.

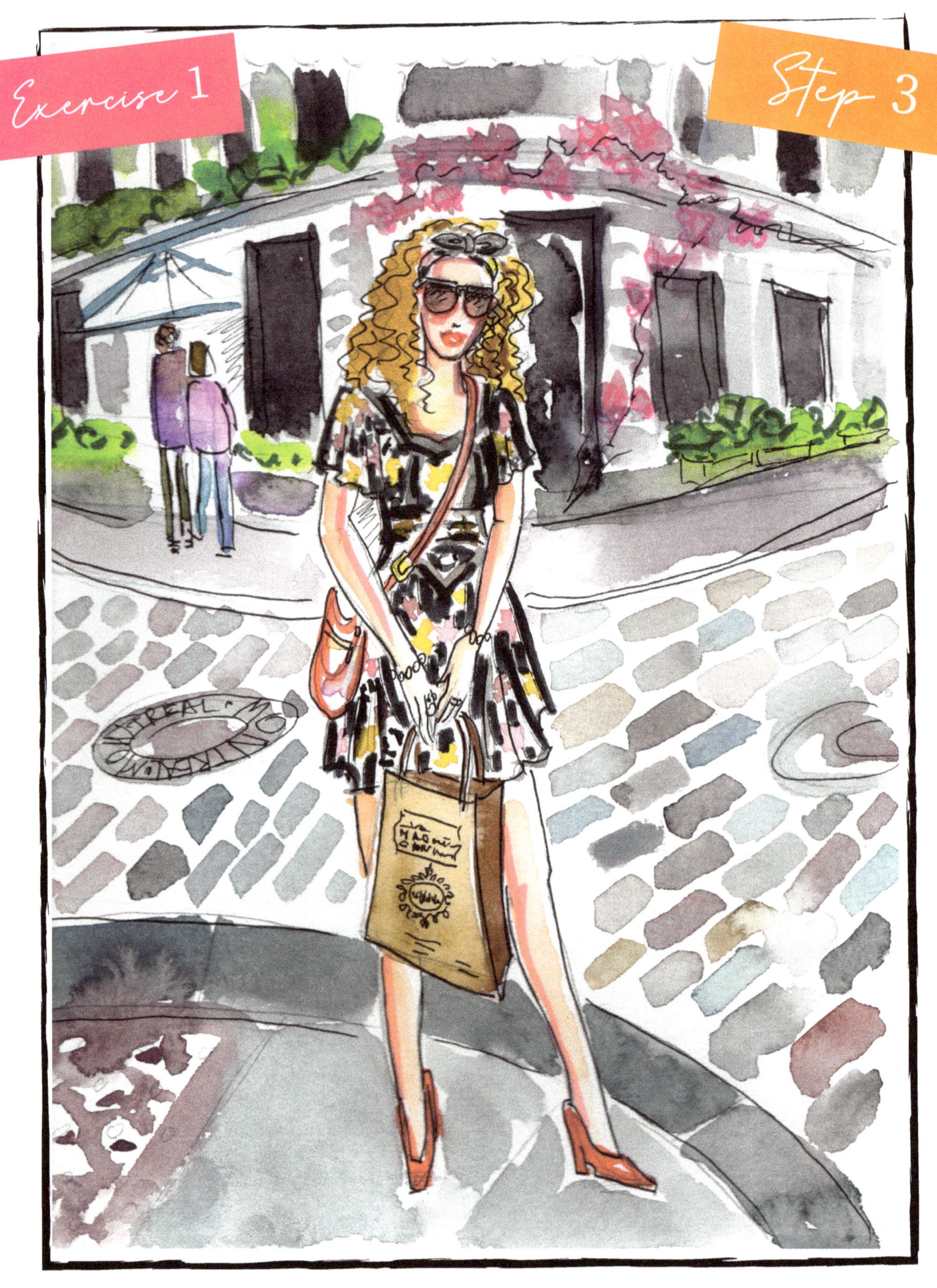

Once your first layer of watercolor dries, add some shading layers and details. When this layer dries, add final touches with pens and markers, as shown.

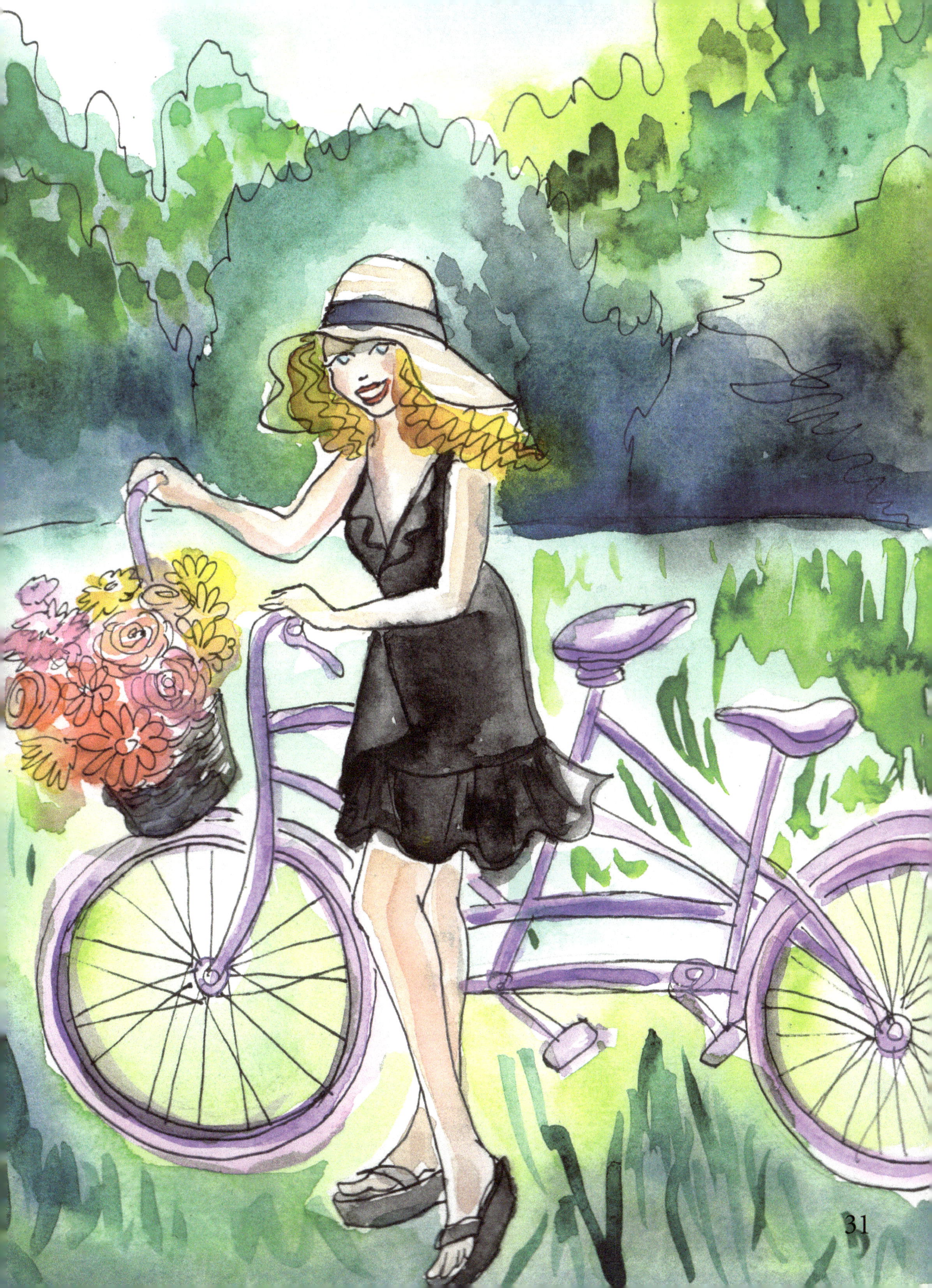

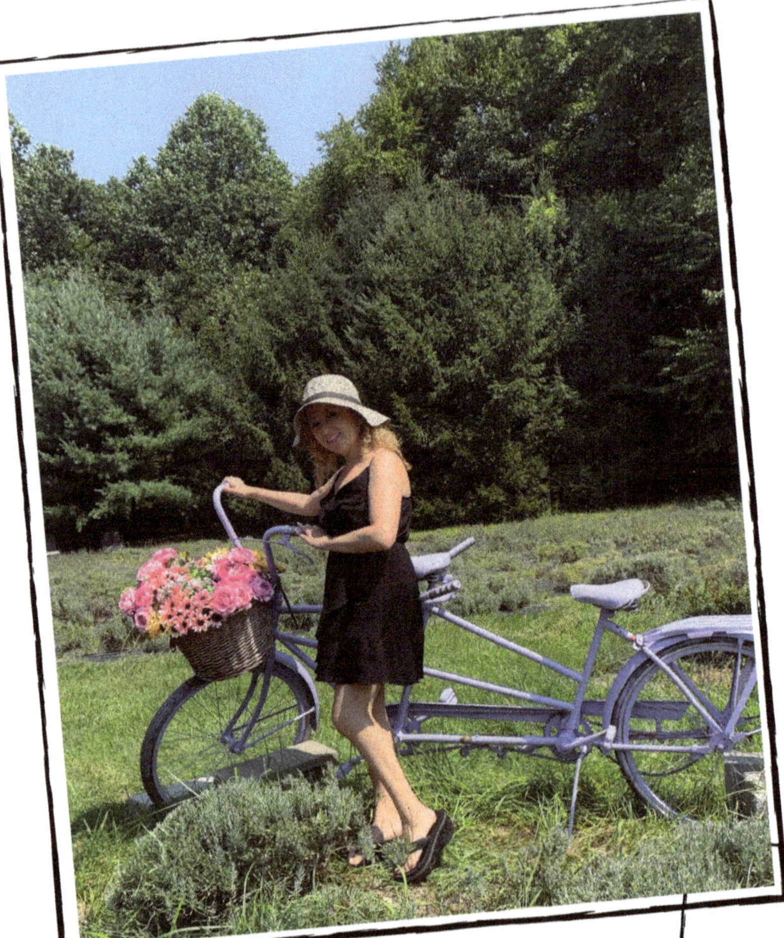

Now, let's work on a simple nature scene. We have some trees in the background, a horizon, a green field in the foreground, with our figure in the middle.

First, sketch the scene with a pencil. You don't need too many details, just placement of the figure. As you can see, I chose to shorten the bicycle, so it fits better into my composition. You can elongate the figure a bit and make the dress and hair flow more. This adds some character to our illustration.

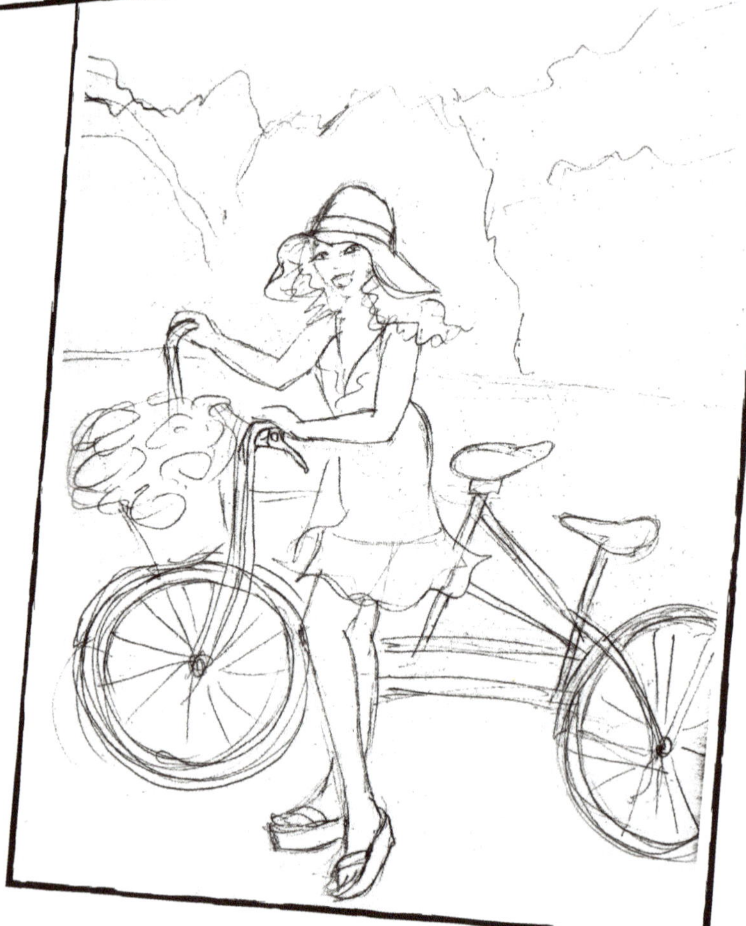

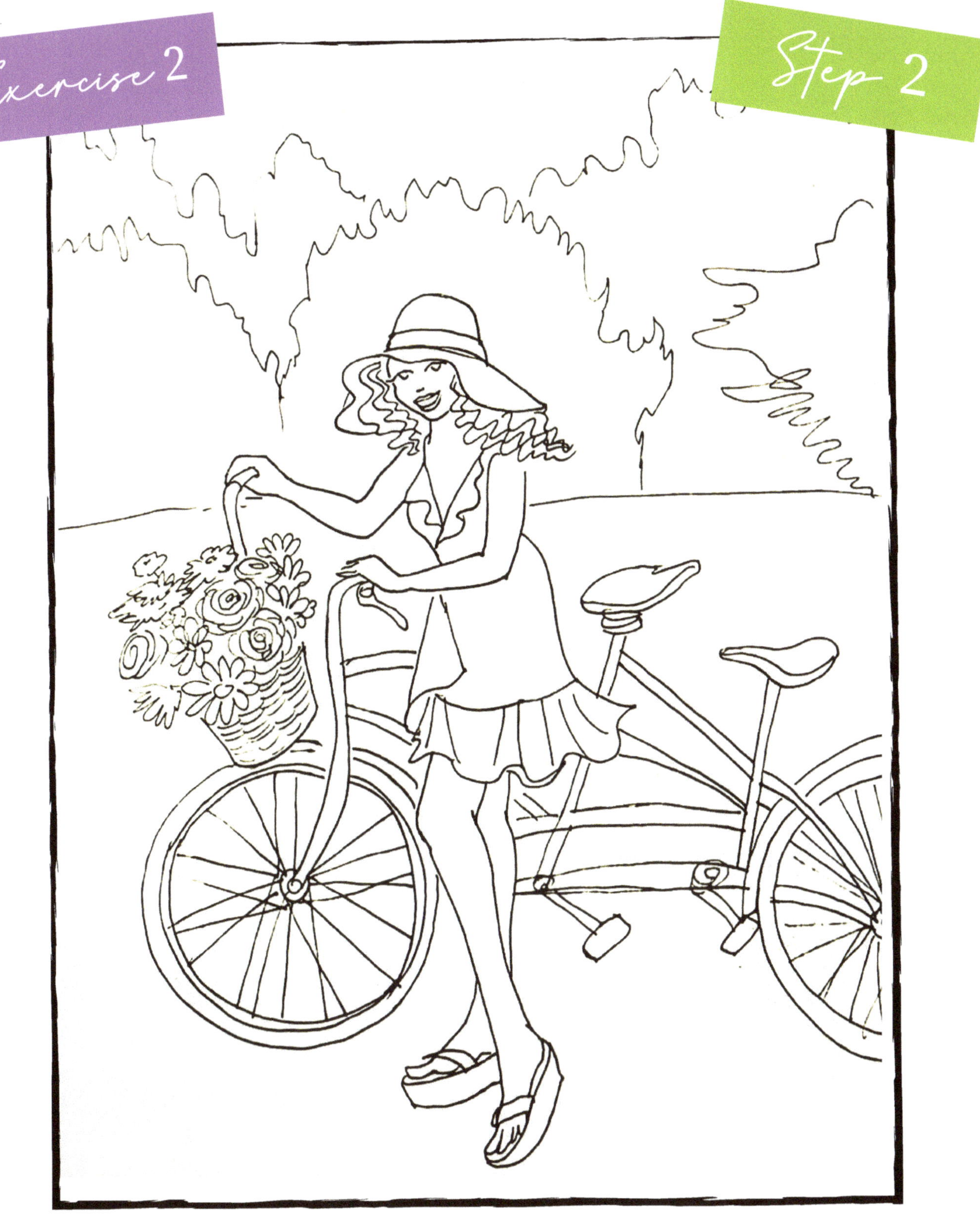

Now let's use art pens to outline and add more details to our sketch. Choose which lines you want to keep and which ones you will erase. Add flower shapes, more bike details, hair, and folds on the clothing. Once you are happy with your outlines, let them dry a bit and erase the pencil marks.

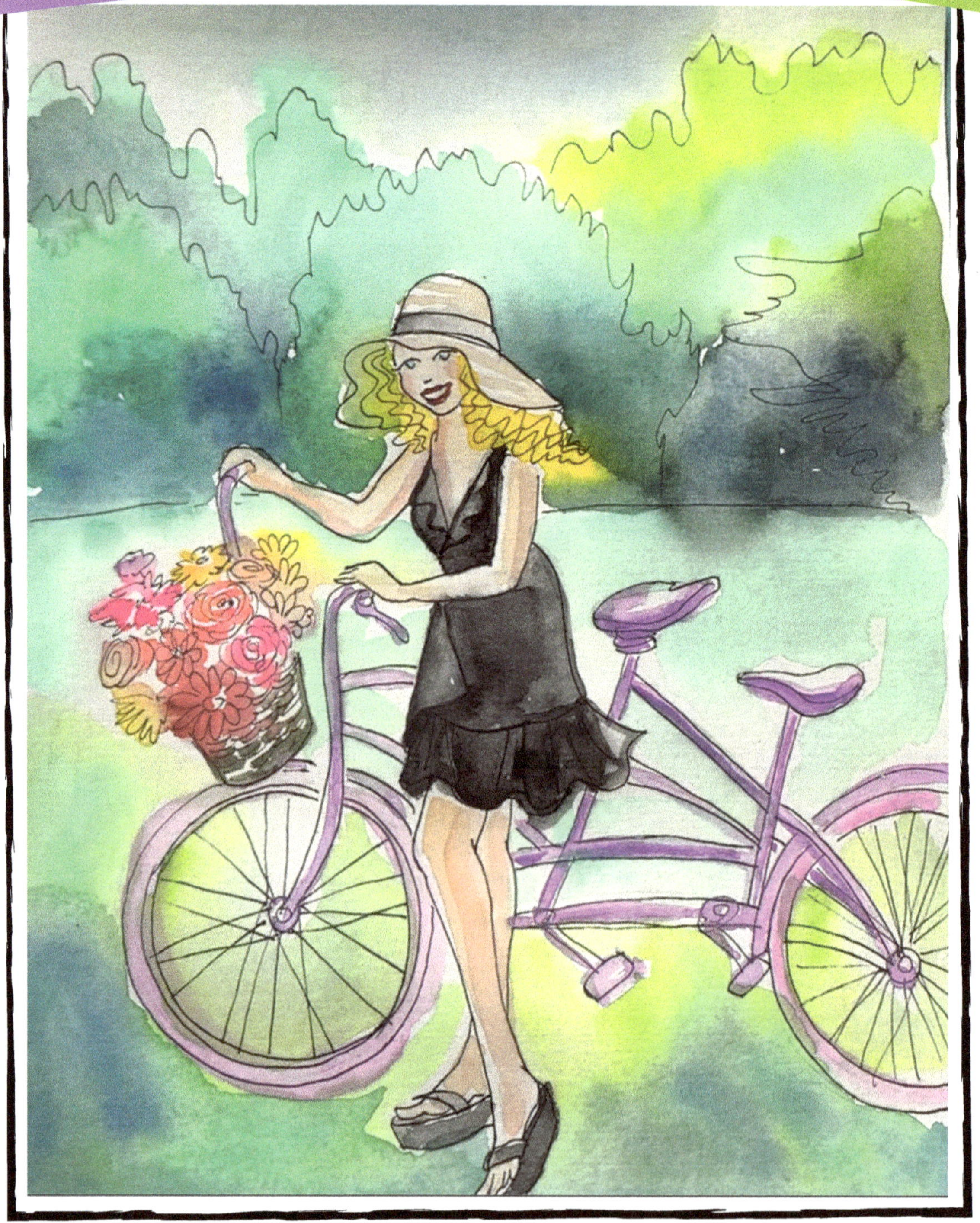

The next step is to apply the watercolors. It does not matter if you paint the figure first or the background, as long as you allow some time for drying, so the colors don't bleed into one another, unless you want them to - like in the areas of dark to light foliage, where it creates quite nice transitions.

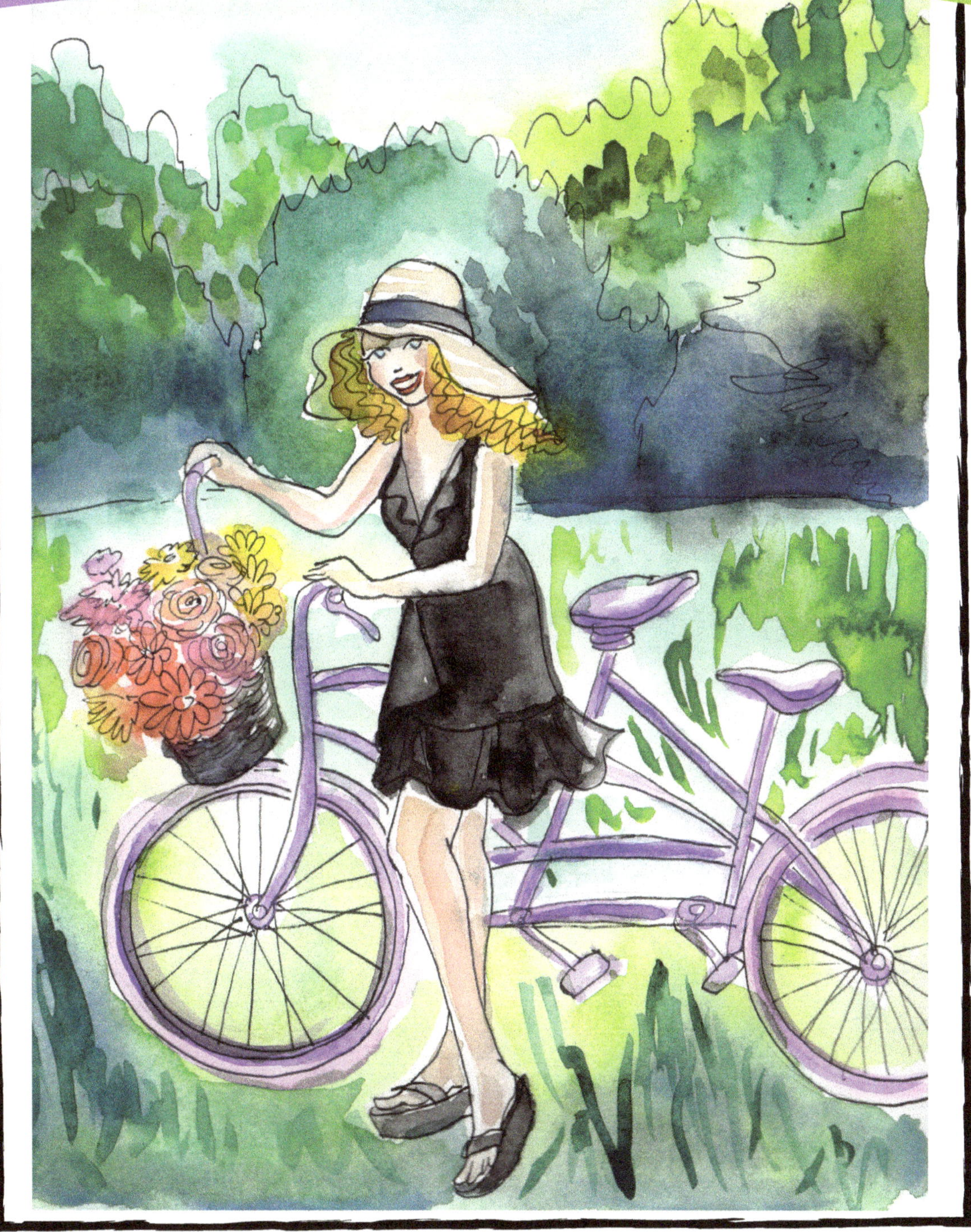

Once your first layer dries, add more depth with additional layers, where applicable. Add grass detail, leaves, shading in the bicycle and the clothes, hair, body and backround. You may dab off extra water where needed, as you work.

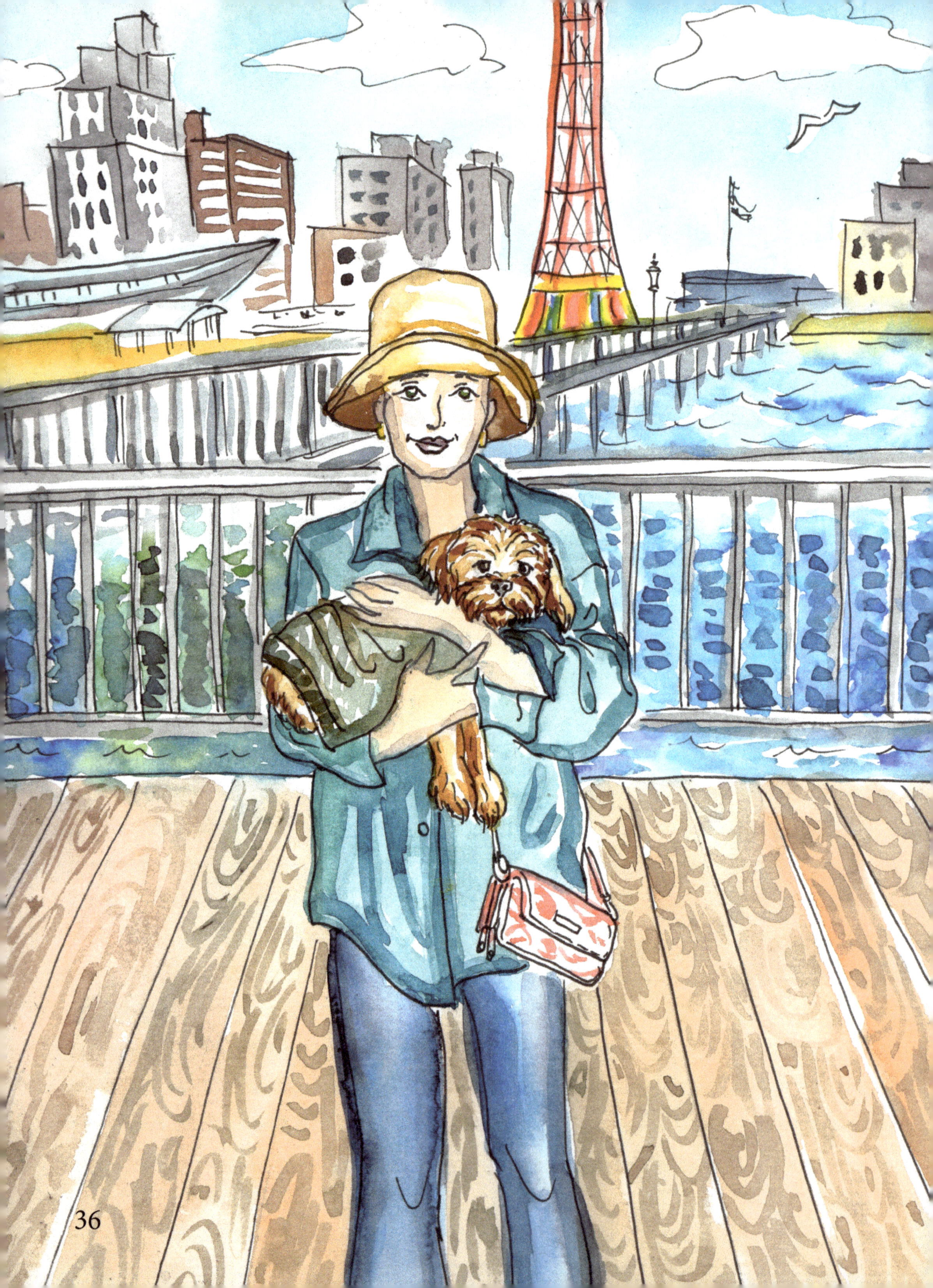

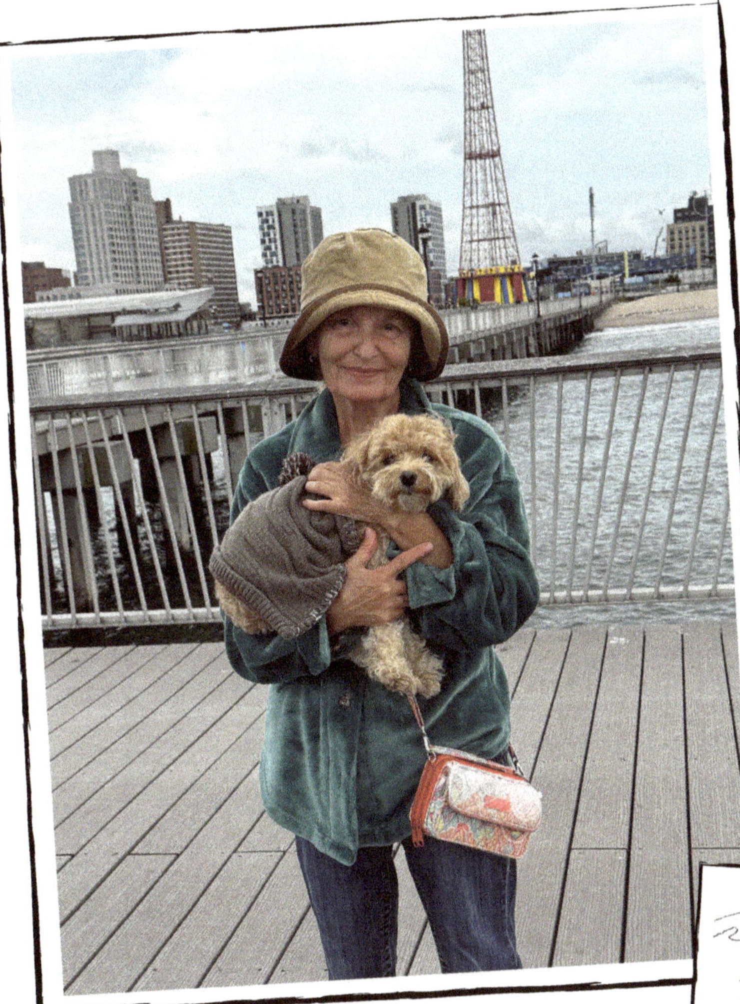

This next example features a figure with a pet. The background is a bit more complex than the previous one. The key here is to give a suggestion of it, without going into too many details.

Let's make a basic sketch. I always start with the figure. When I draw, I pay attention to the figure's position relative to the background objects. For example, where is the top of the head located relative to the background buildings? I tried to simplify the lines of the deck and the fence for this image. Remember, you can edit your photo reference, to suit your needs.

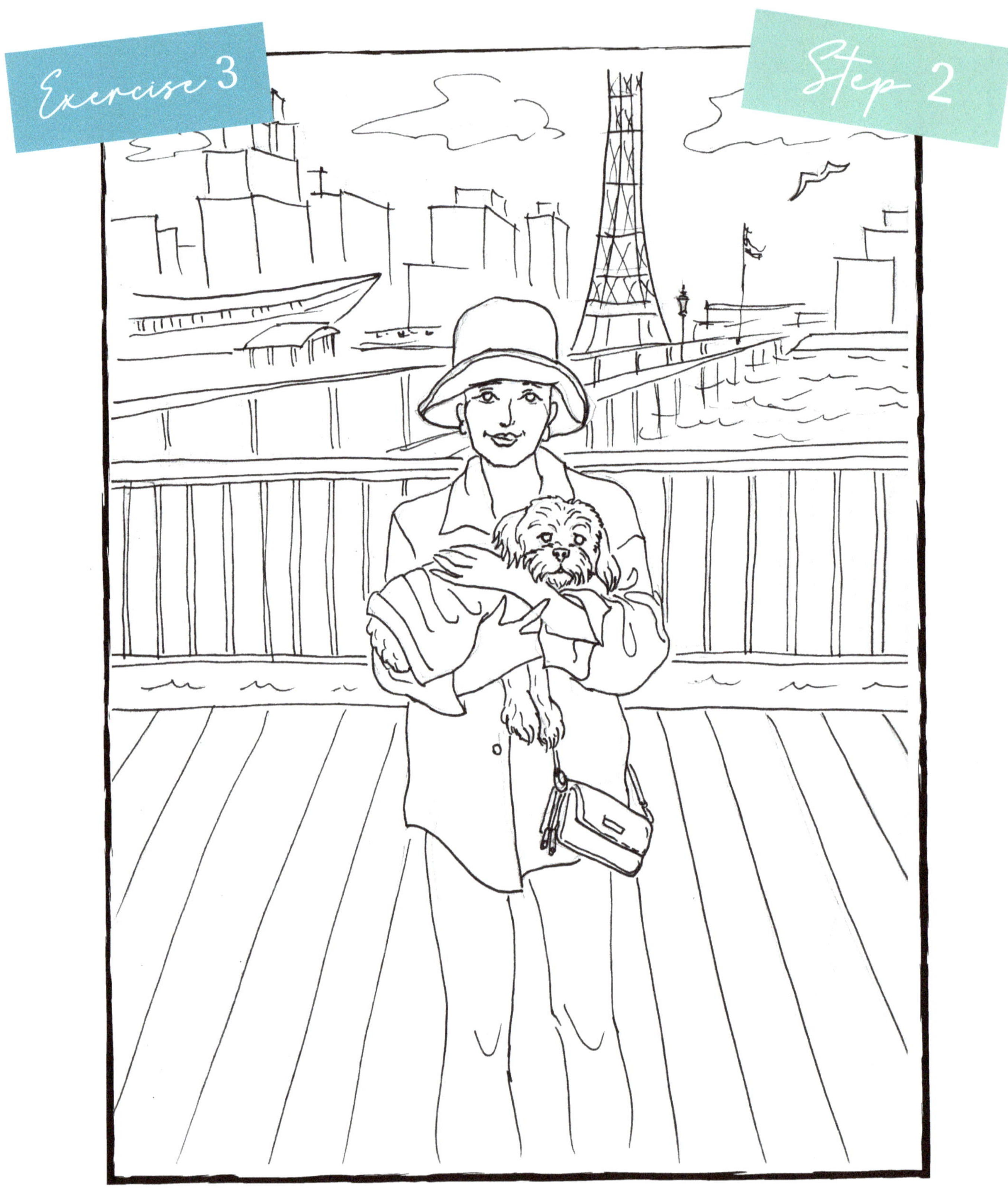

Use pens to outline and add more details to your sketch.
Choose which lines you want to keep and which ones you
will erase. Add dog fur, clothing folds, waves, indicate buildings,
beams, flags, lamps, etc. Lastly, erase pencil lines to clean it up.

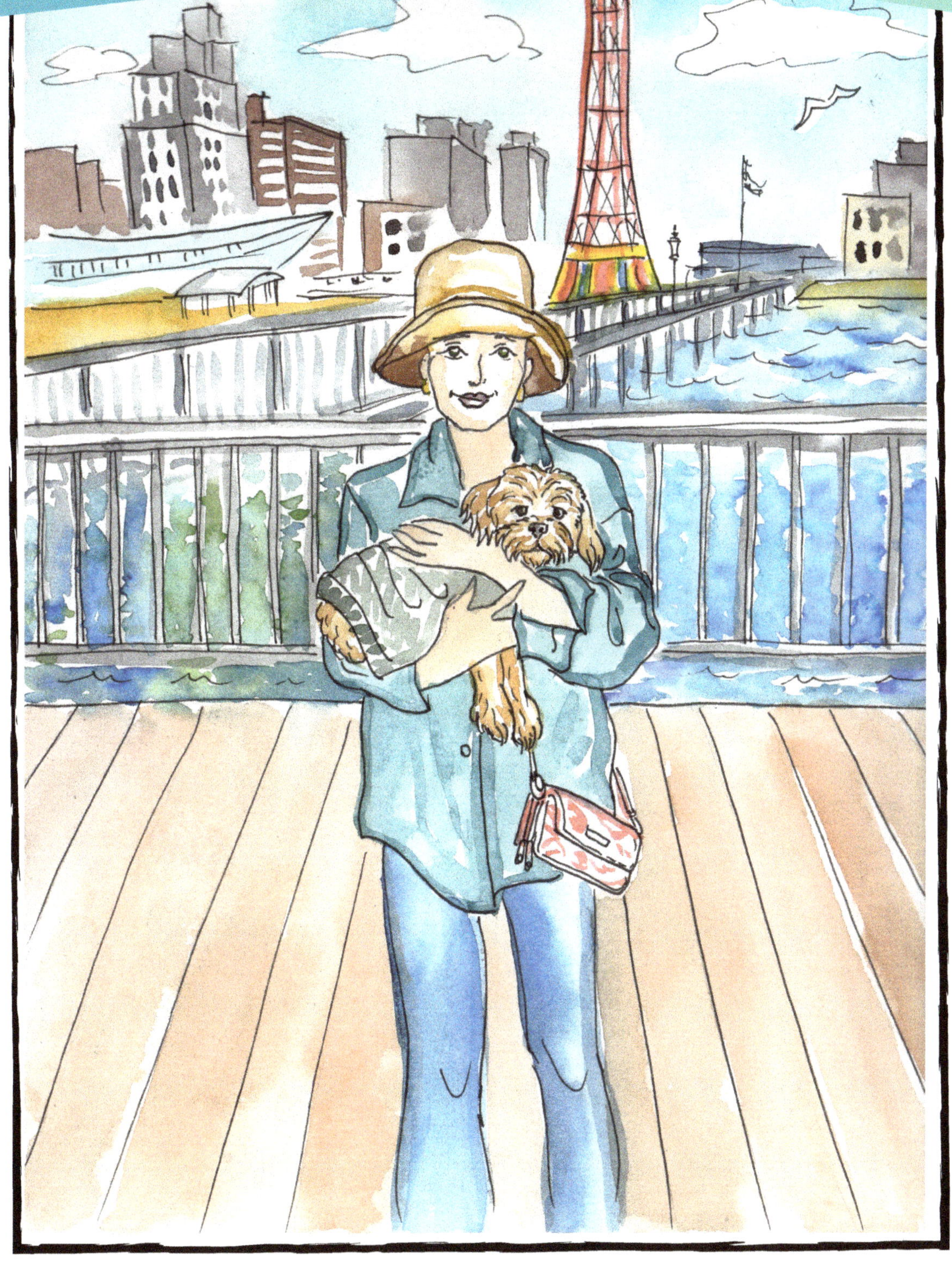

Now add the watercolors. Use a vibrant, happy pallet.
Vary brush widths for larger and smaller details.
When painting the ocean and sky, let colors bleed a bit
into one another.

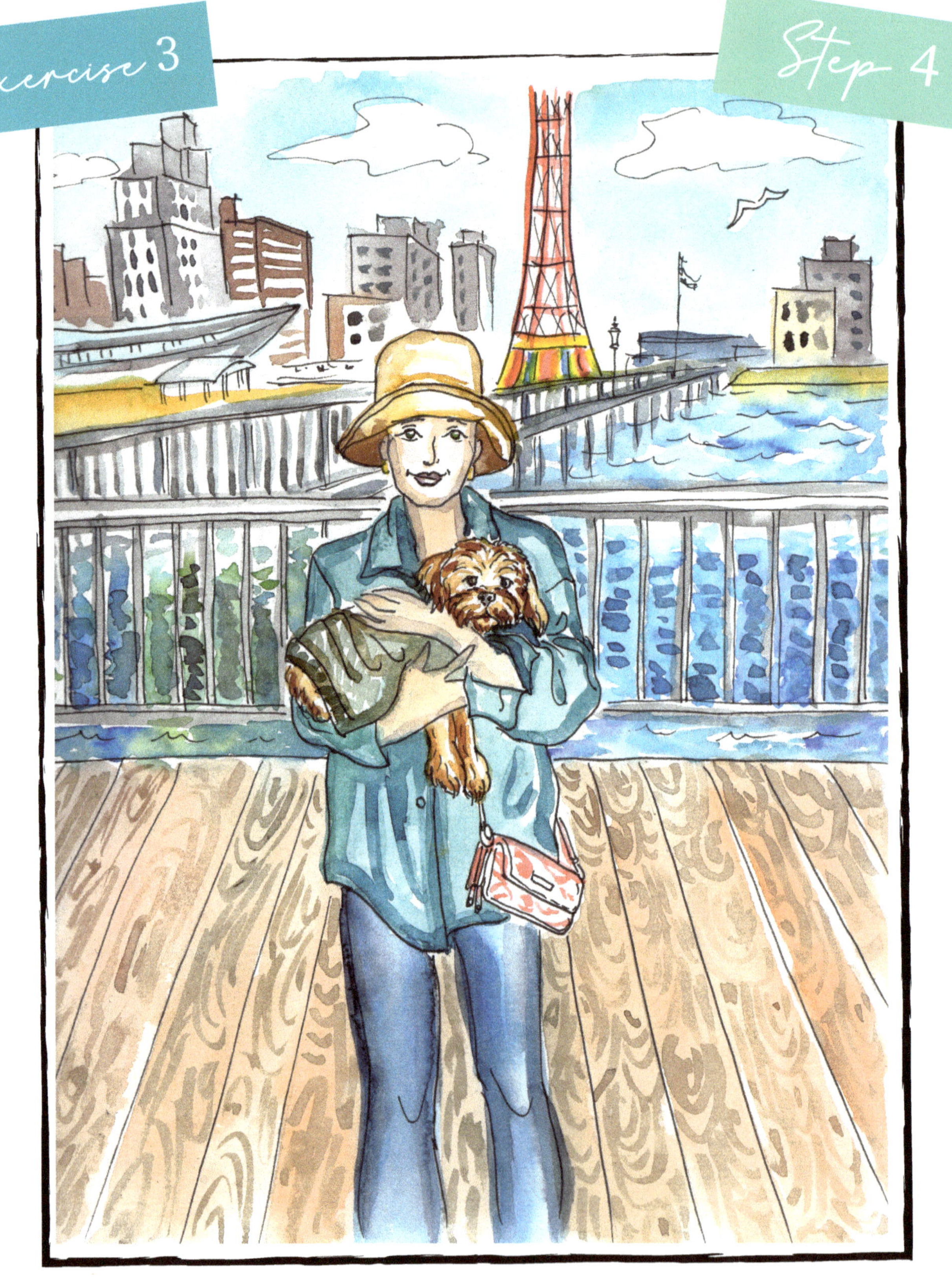

When the first layer dries, add more details and shading. Pay attention to the wood beam patters, water, dog fur, clothing folds. Indicate windows and other background details.

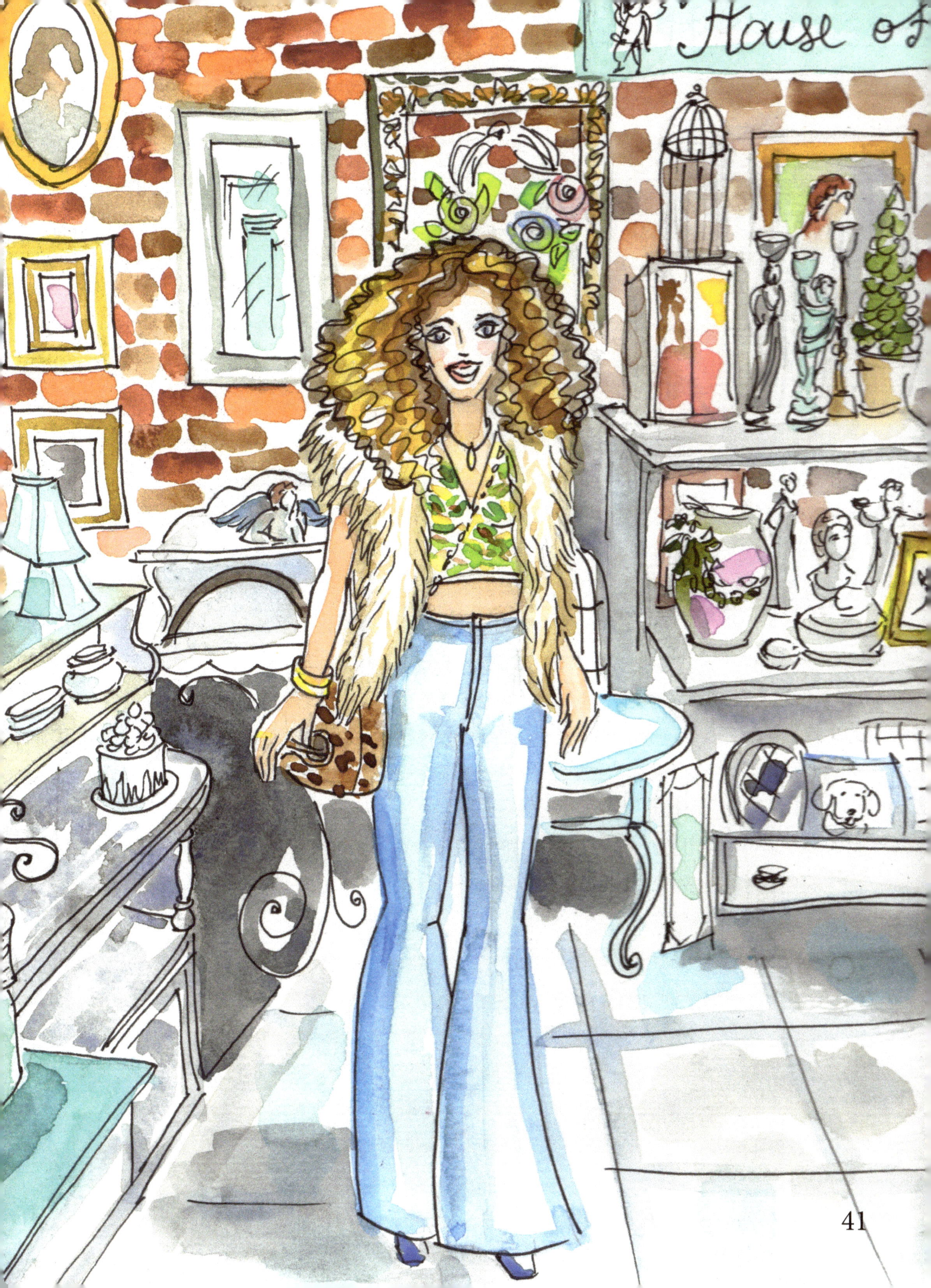

House of

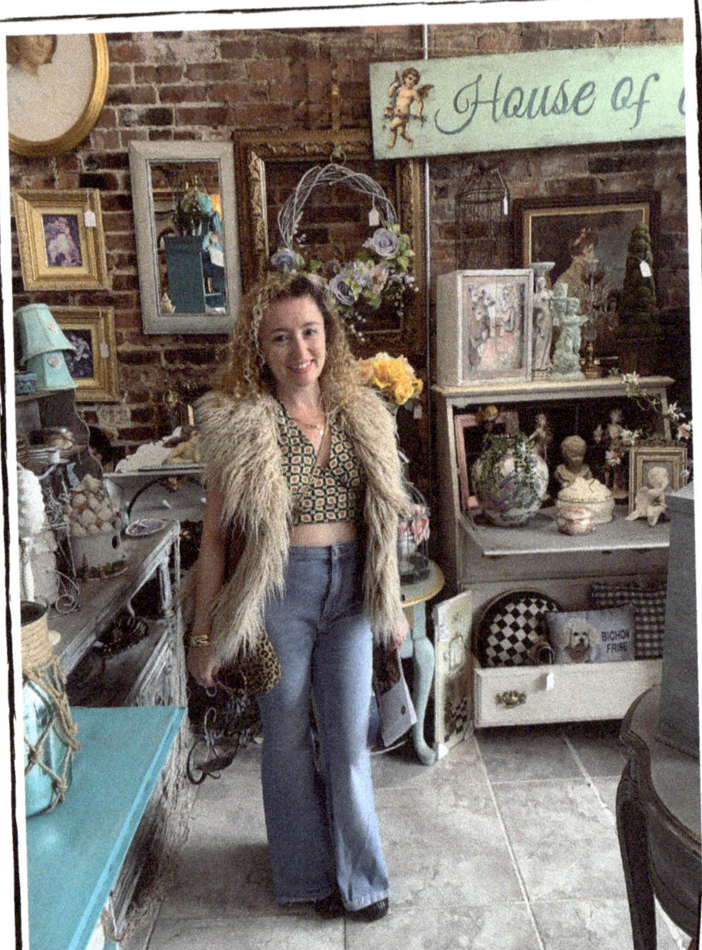

For this exercise, let us explore drawing a fashion composition with a really detailed interior background. Here is a photo of our model in an antique store. This illustration will be designed to show off the interesting interior of the store.

First, we will create a sketch using a pencil. Do not get into too many details at this stage. We want to portray the general layout and feel of the store. I have placed the model at the center of the composition, making sure that her head and feet fit, with ample room to show the wall, decor, frames, mirrors, flowers, furniture, and more.

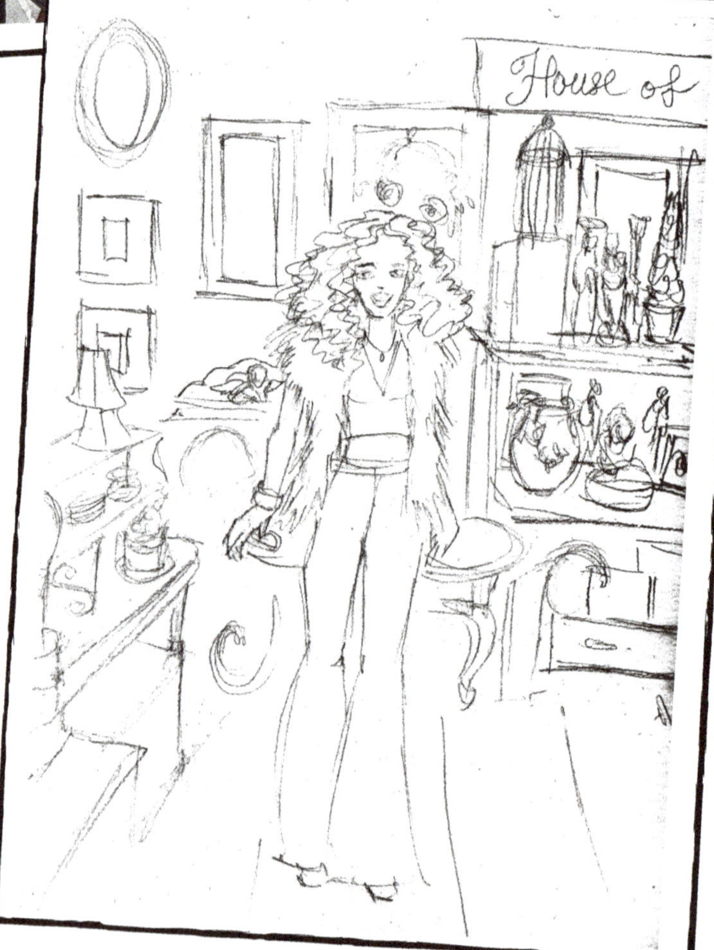

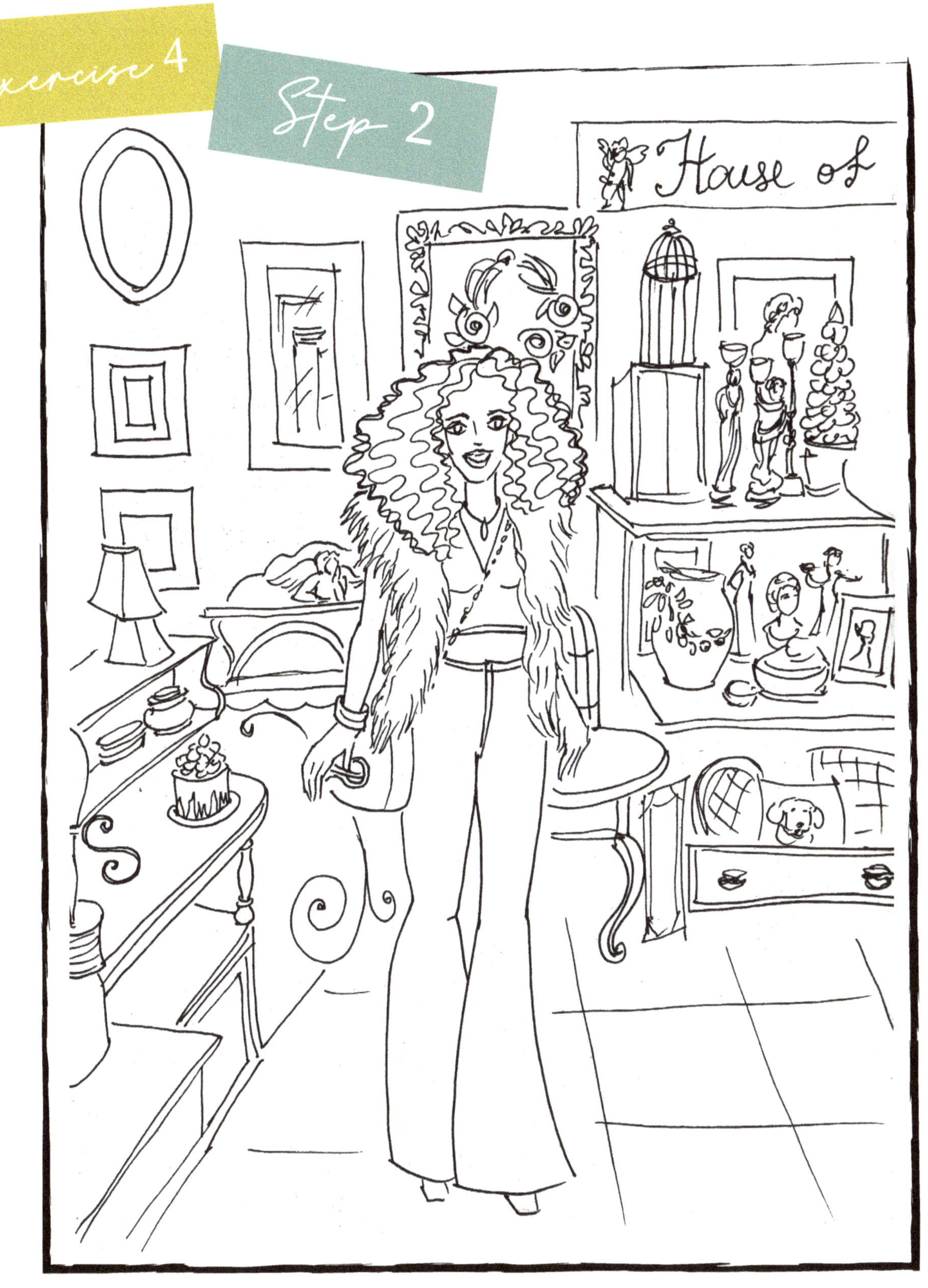

After you have sketched your composition in pencil, use a black art pen or a waterproof ink pen to outline the parts you wish to remain in your drawing. Then erase the pencil lines. At this stage you can add more details and elements you wish to emphasize.

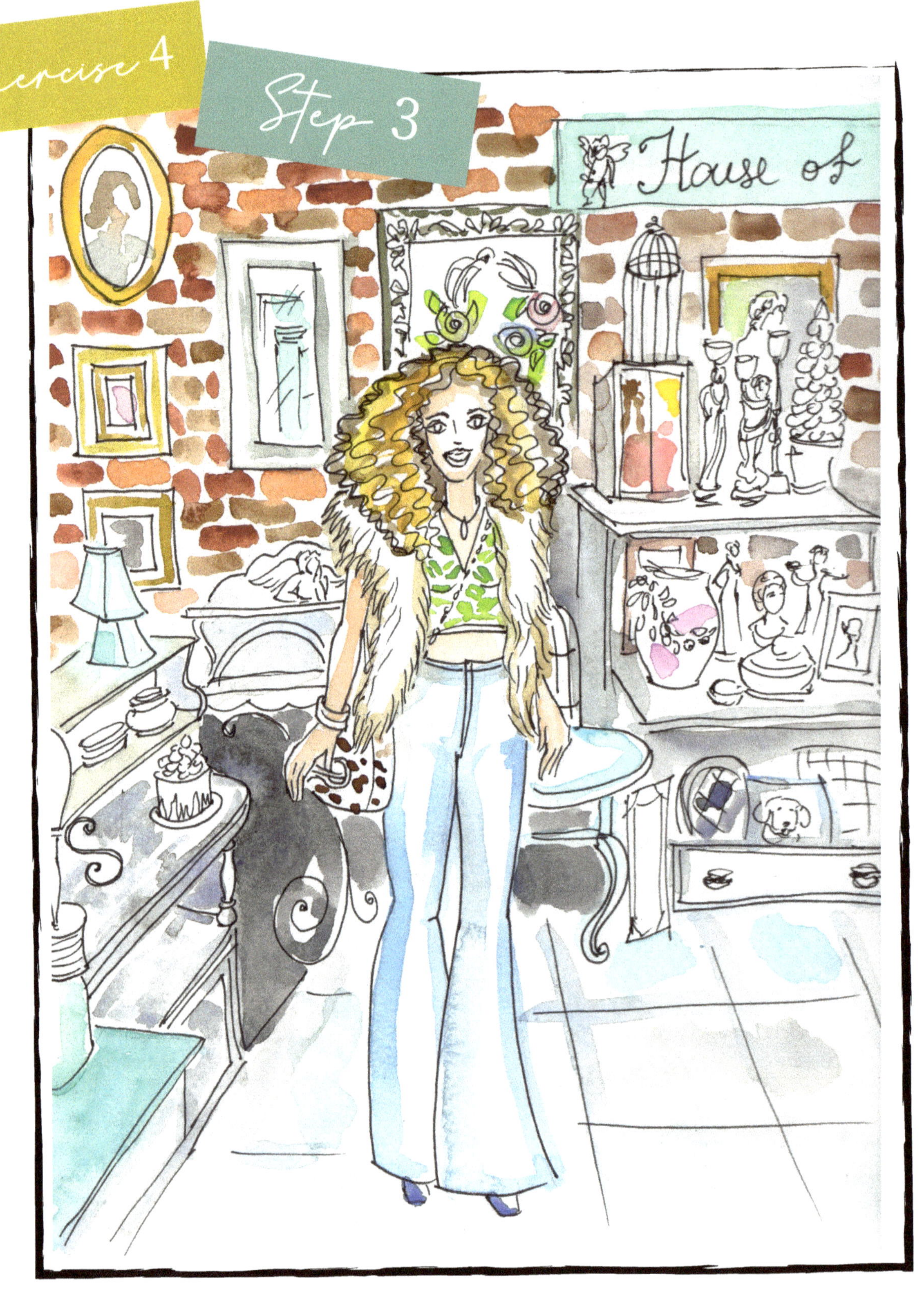

Now, let's paint our first watercolor layer. Use simple and clean colors, dabbing off extra water. Pay attention to interesting details, like the rustic brick wall. You can vary the colors of the bricks, to make them more textured and interesting.

44

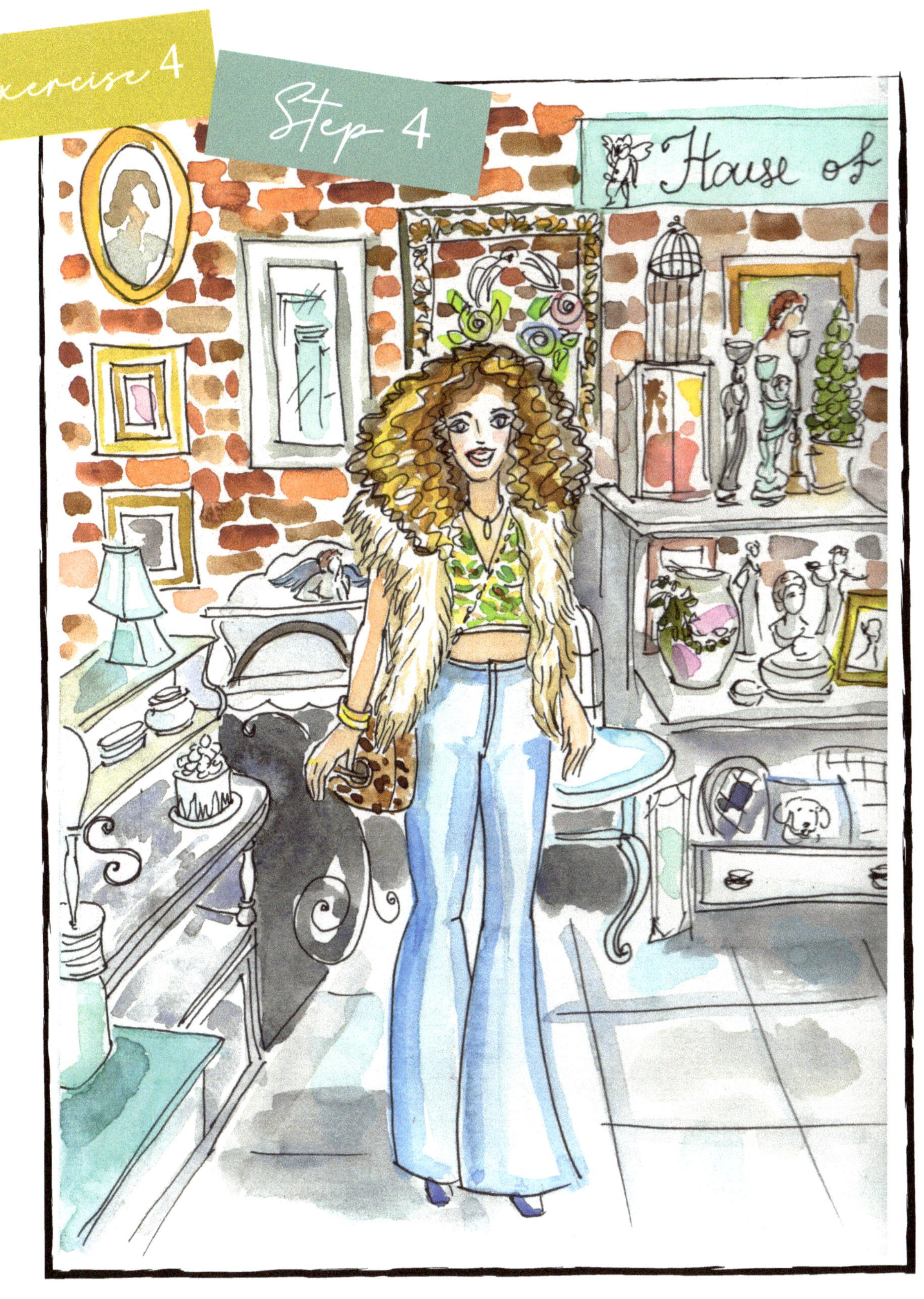

Once the first layer dries, now go in to add more shading and details to your painting. The painting should get more saturated and have more depth at this stage.

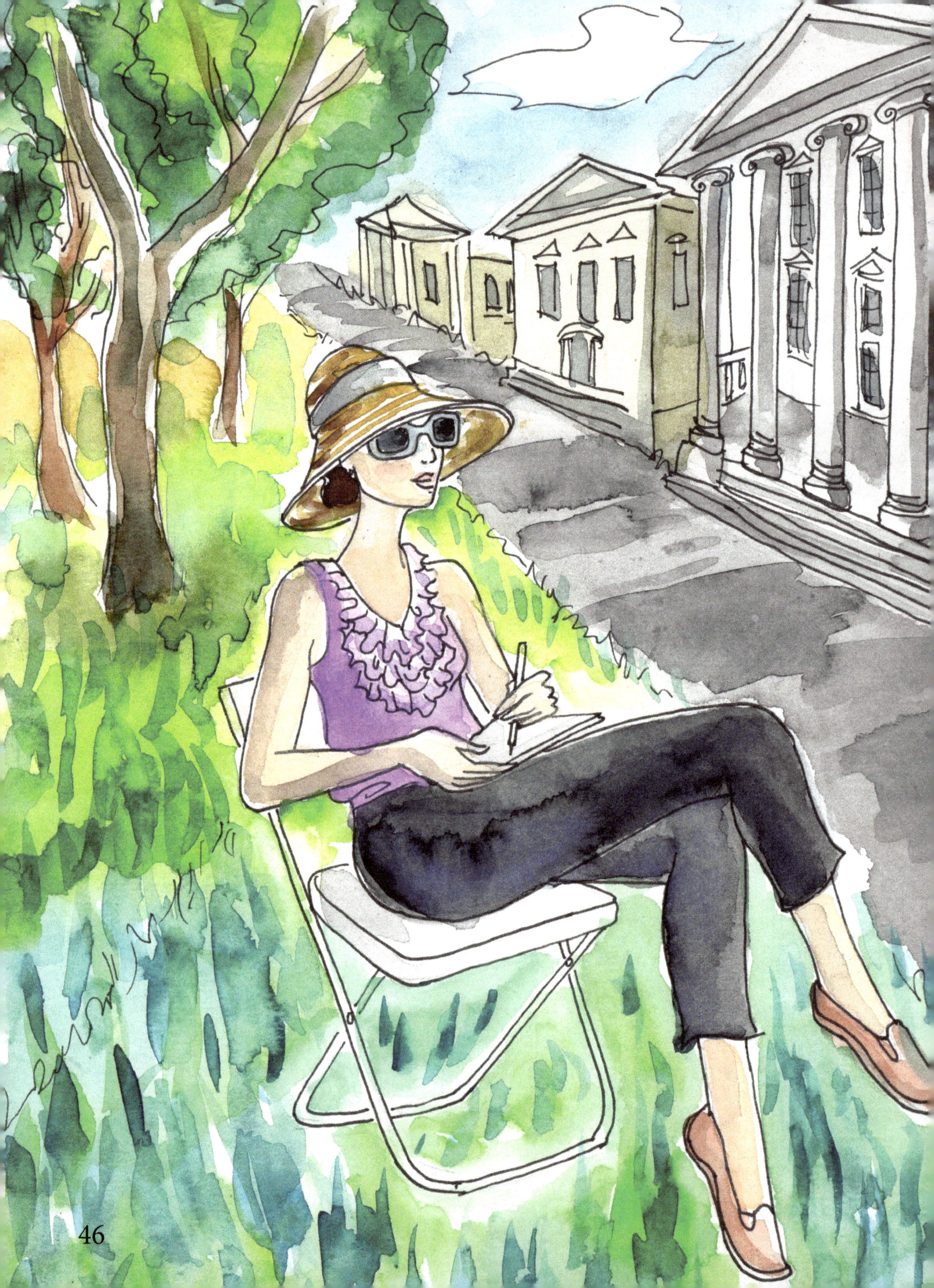

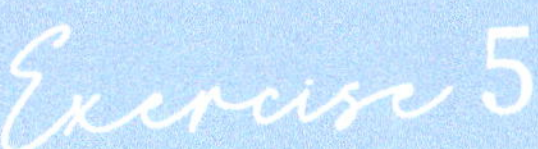

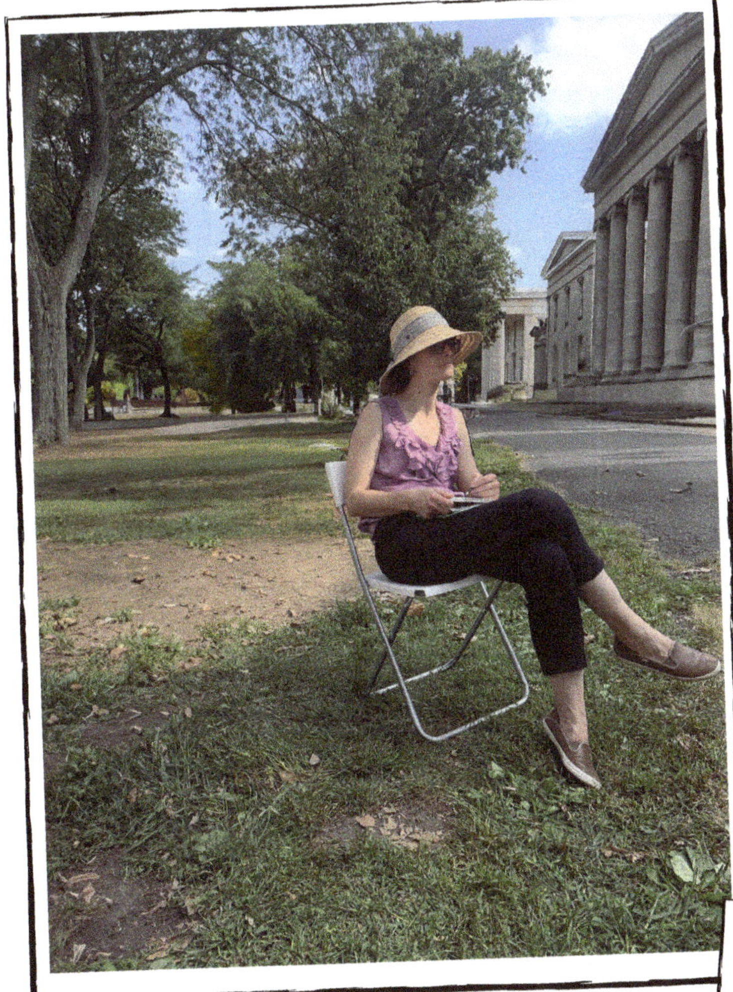

Here, the figure is seated on a chair in the foreground, within a park scenery, with trees on one side and buildings on the other side, getting visually smaller as they get further away. You can slightly modify the drawing to fit your goals.

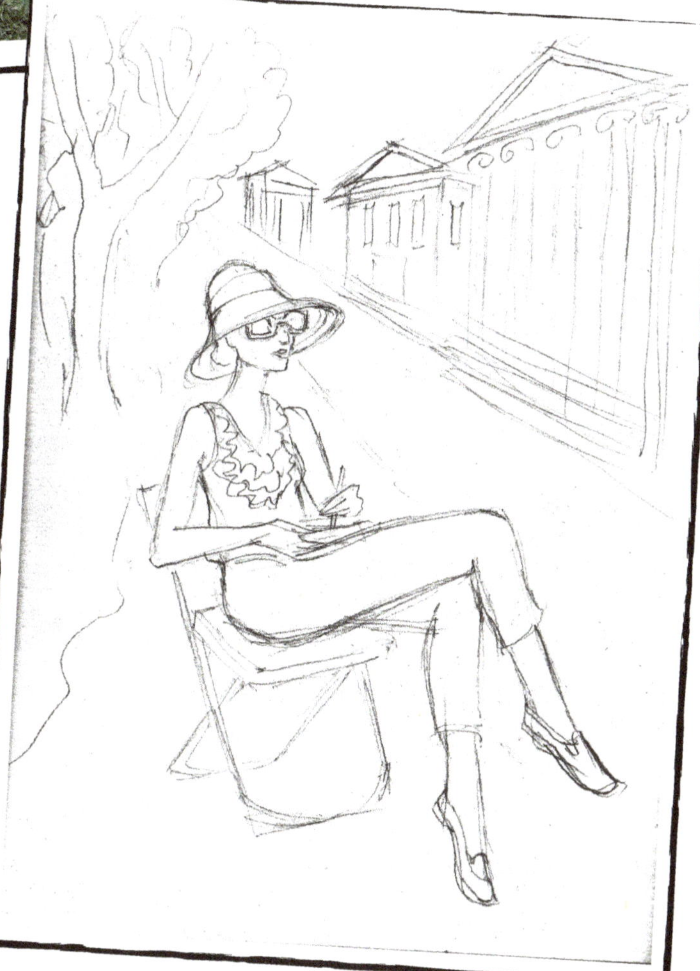

I have made the figure more central to the composition. I have also added more of the buildings, to balance the scene. The tree in the background is now a bit closer to the figure. When you draw, feel free to make your fashion figures more expressive. Our model is already tall and lean, so not much exaggeration is needed.

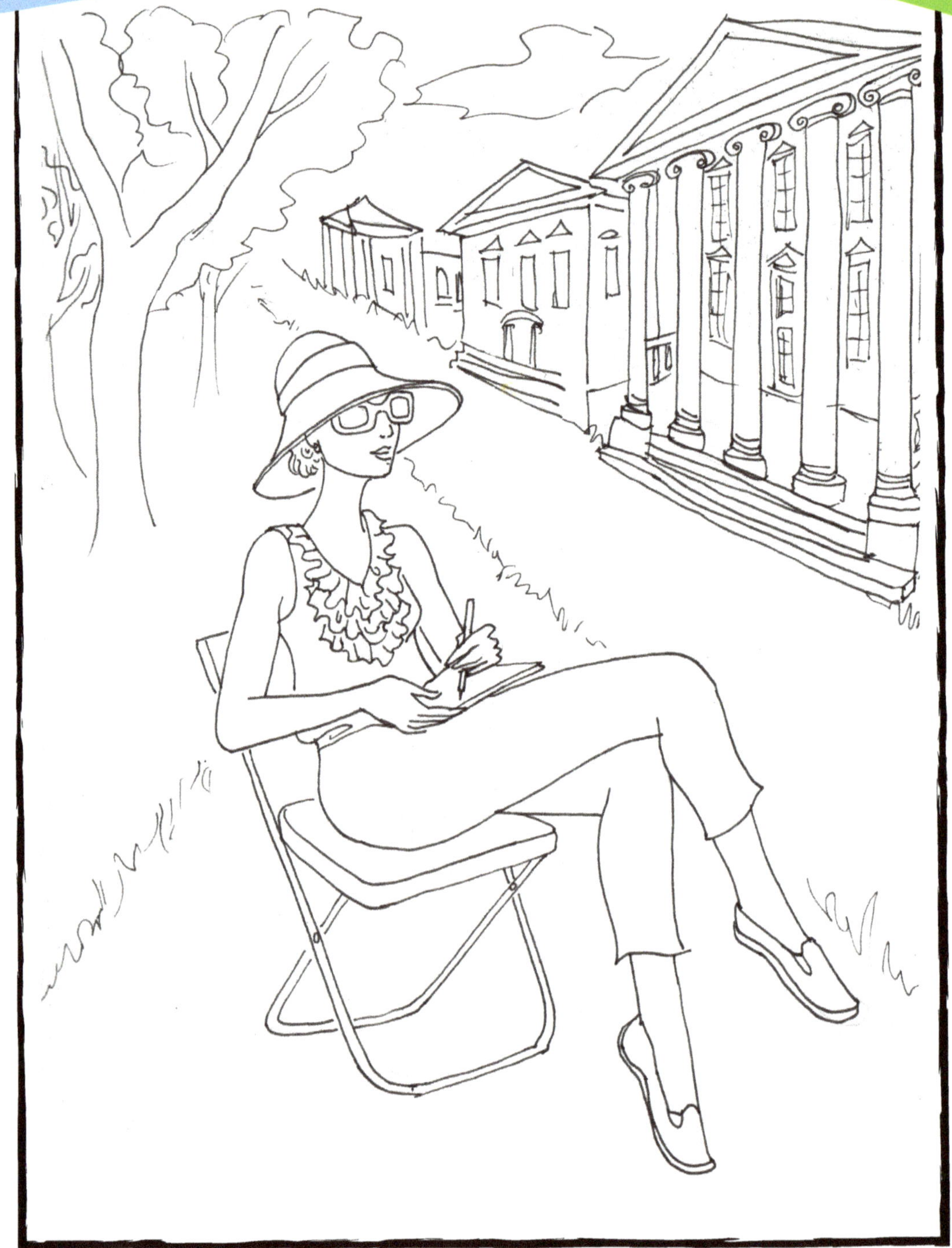

Step two is to outline our drawing with a pen or thin marker. This is an optional step, when you want your drawing/painting to look more sharp and defined. Select what you would like to keep, and erase the rest of the pencil lines.

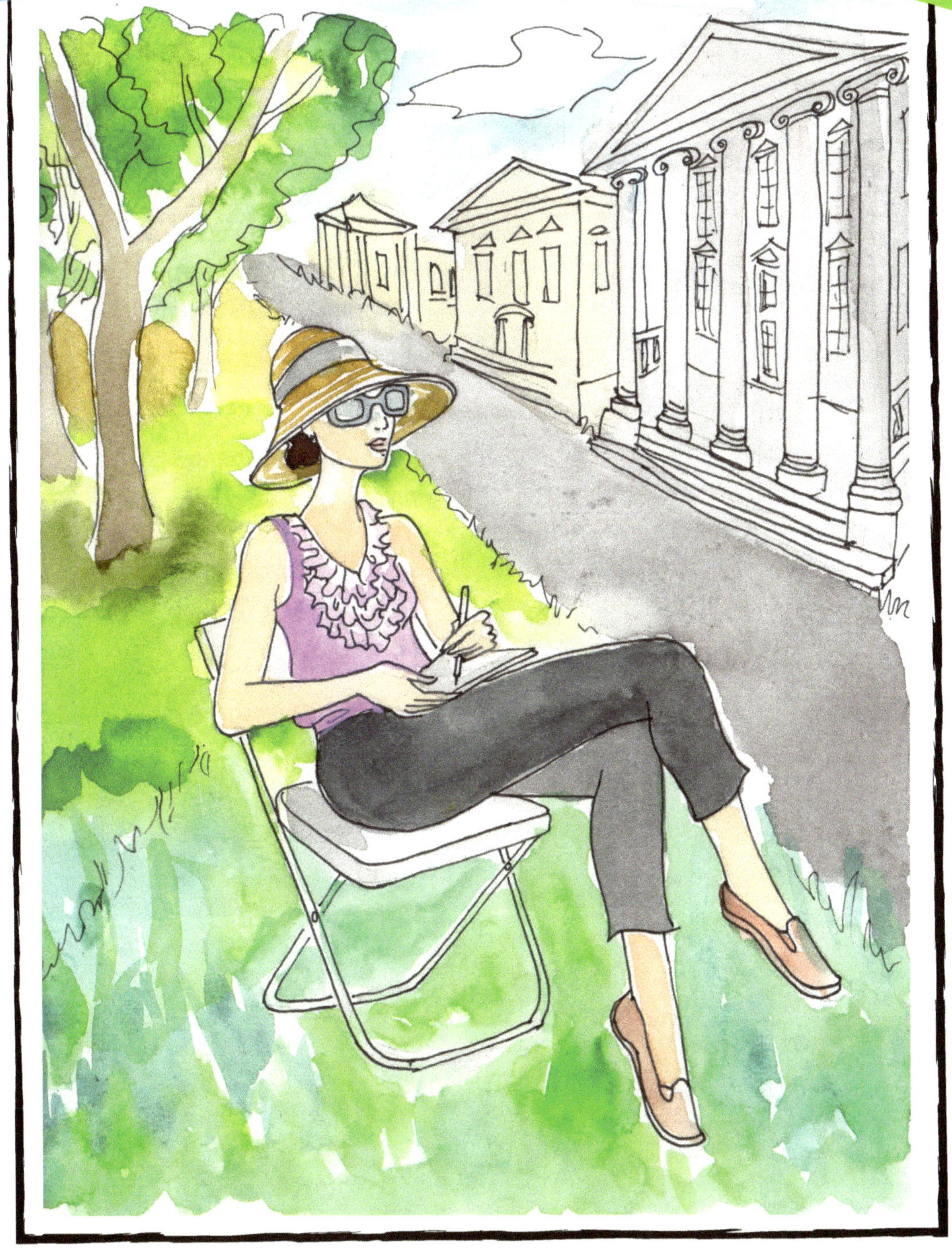

Now paint your first layer of watercolor. In areas like grass and foliage, let the colors bleed into one another, to showcase the painterly watercolor properties. Where you wish to have a more controlled color, dab off the extra water with a tissue.

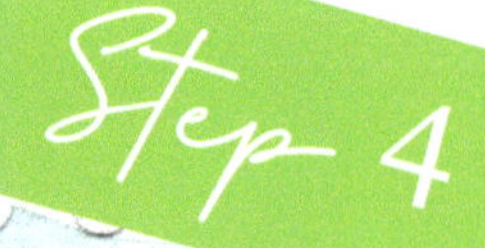

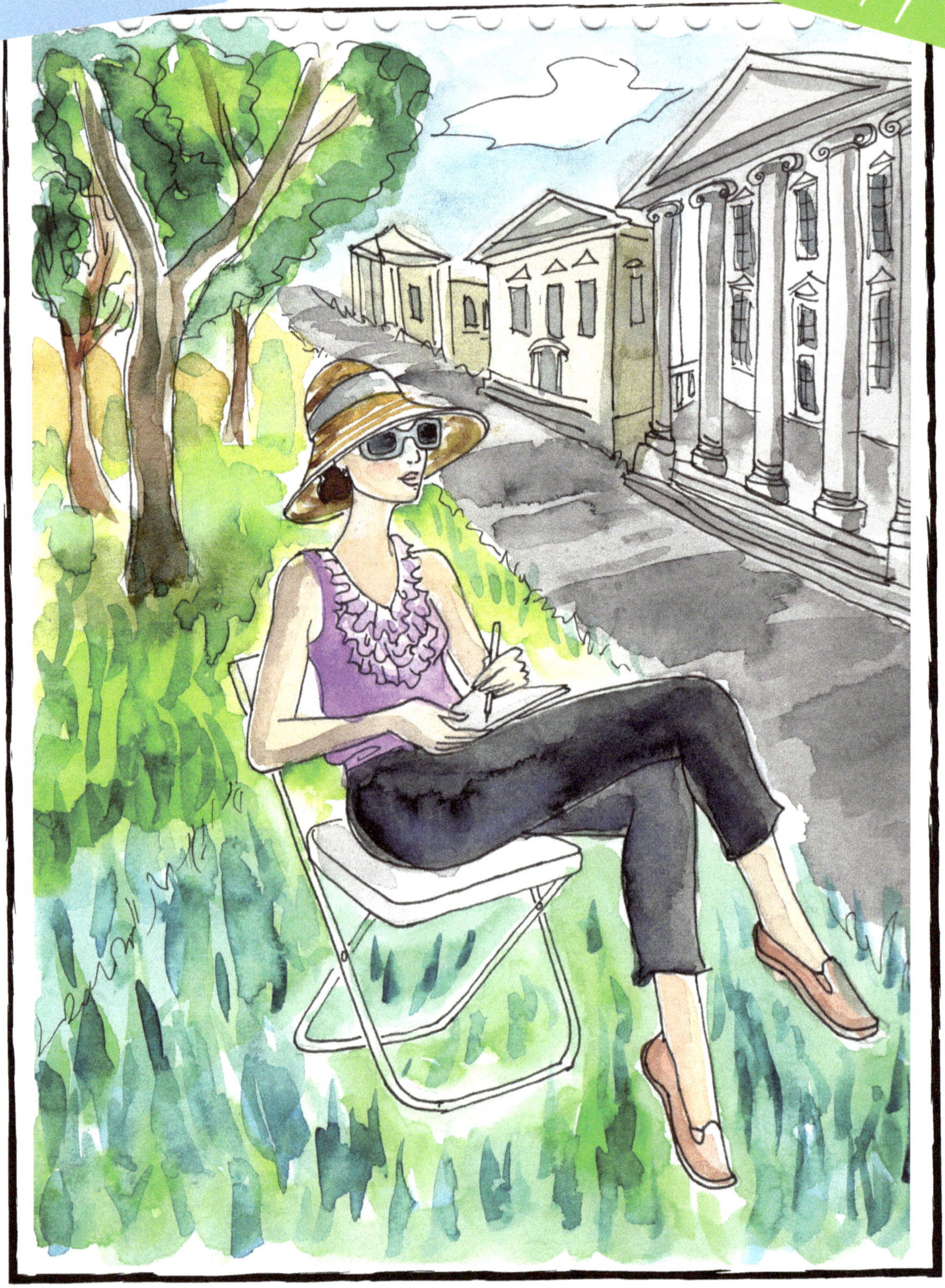

When your first watercolor layer has dried, you can add more detail with additional watercolor. Here I added blades of grass, some more shading to the model, pavement and buildings.

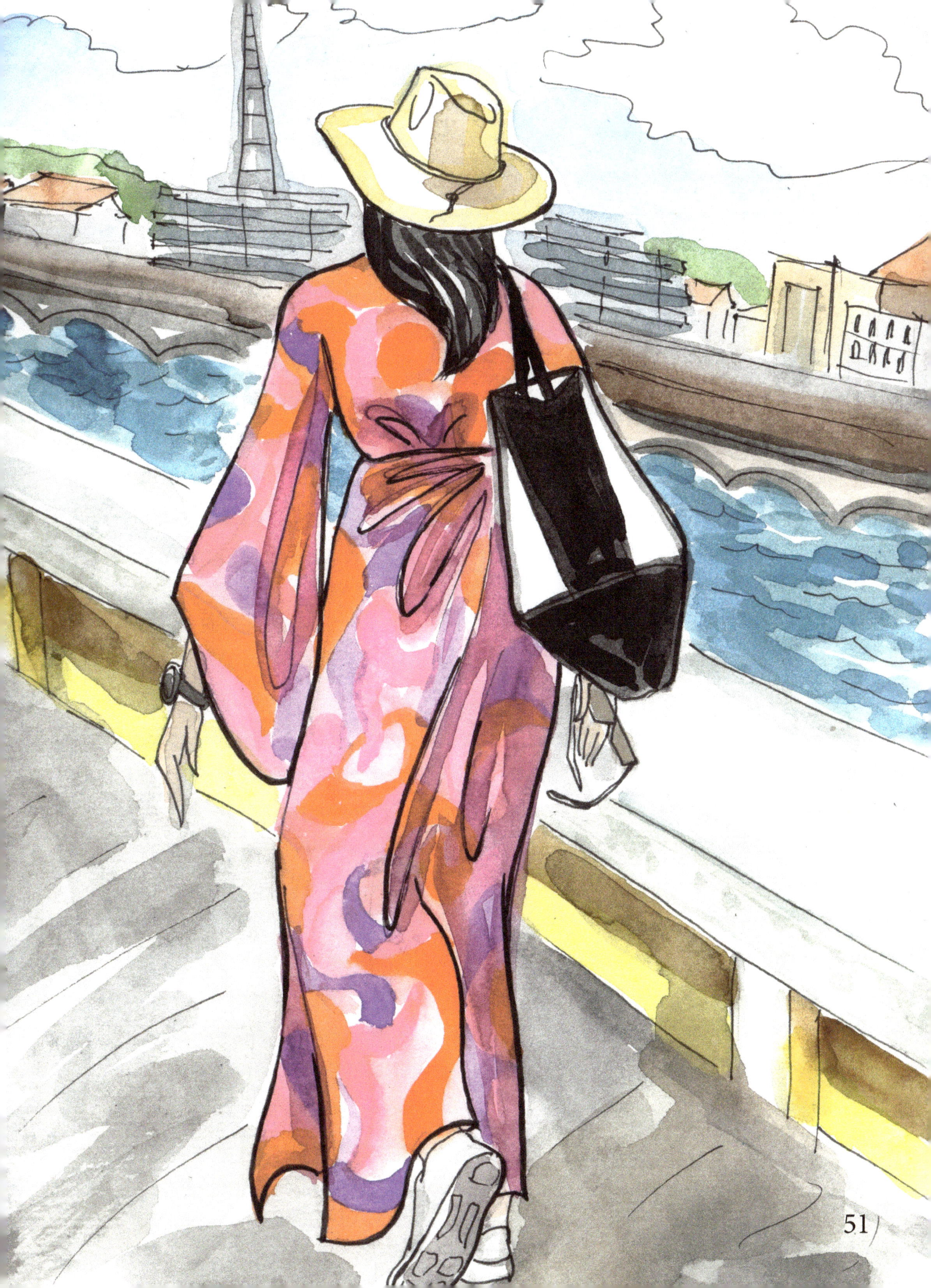

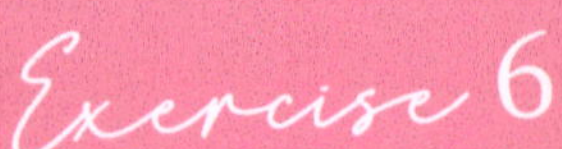

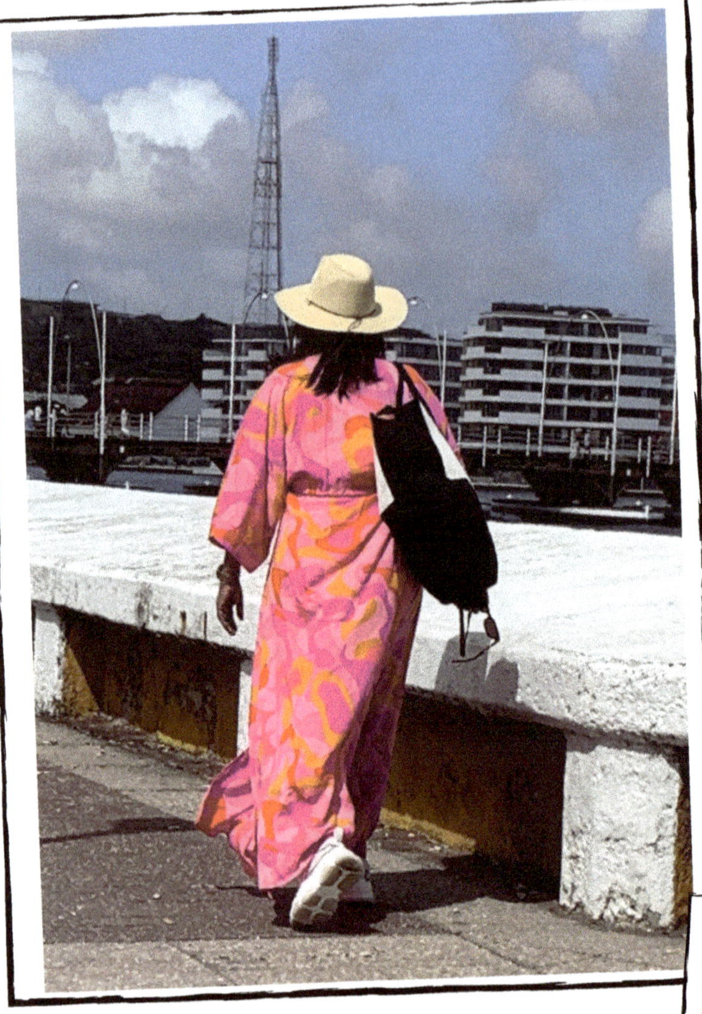

In this example, we will draw and paint a woman walking along the promenade.
She has on a beautiful flowing cover-up, which is perfect for our street fashion exercise. Here we can also practice drawing a figure with a perspective background.

When you make your pencil sketch, place the figure in the center and make her prominent. Indicate fabric folds, and add flow to her garment to show wind and movement.
When you draw a walking figure, try and show the bottom of her shoe, as she makes a stride.
Copy this image to practice.

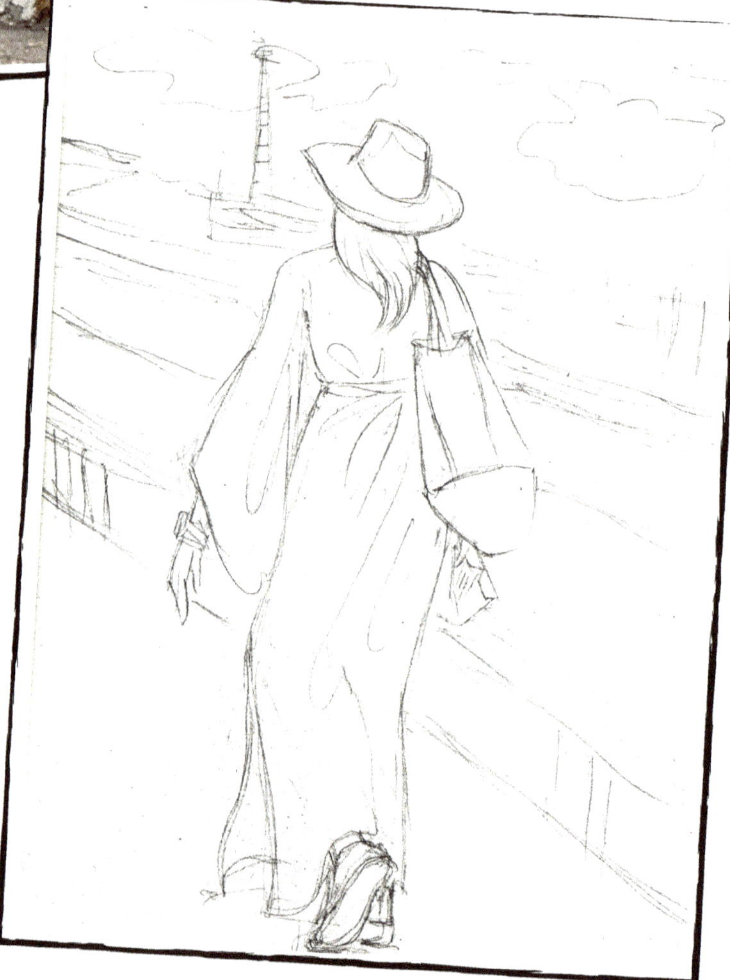

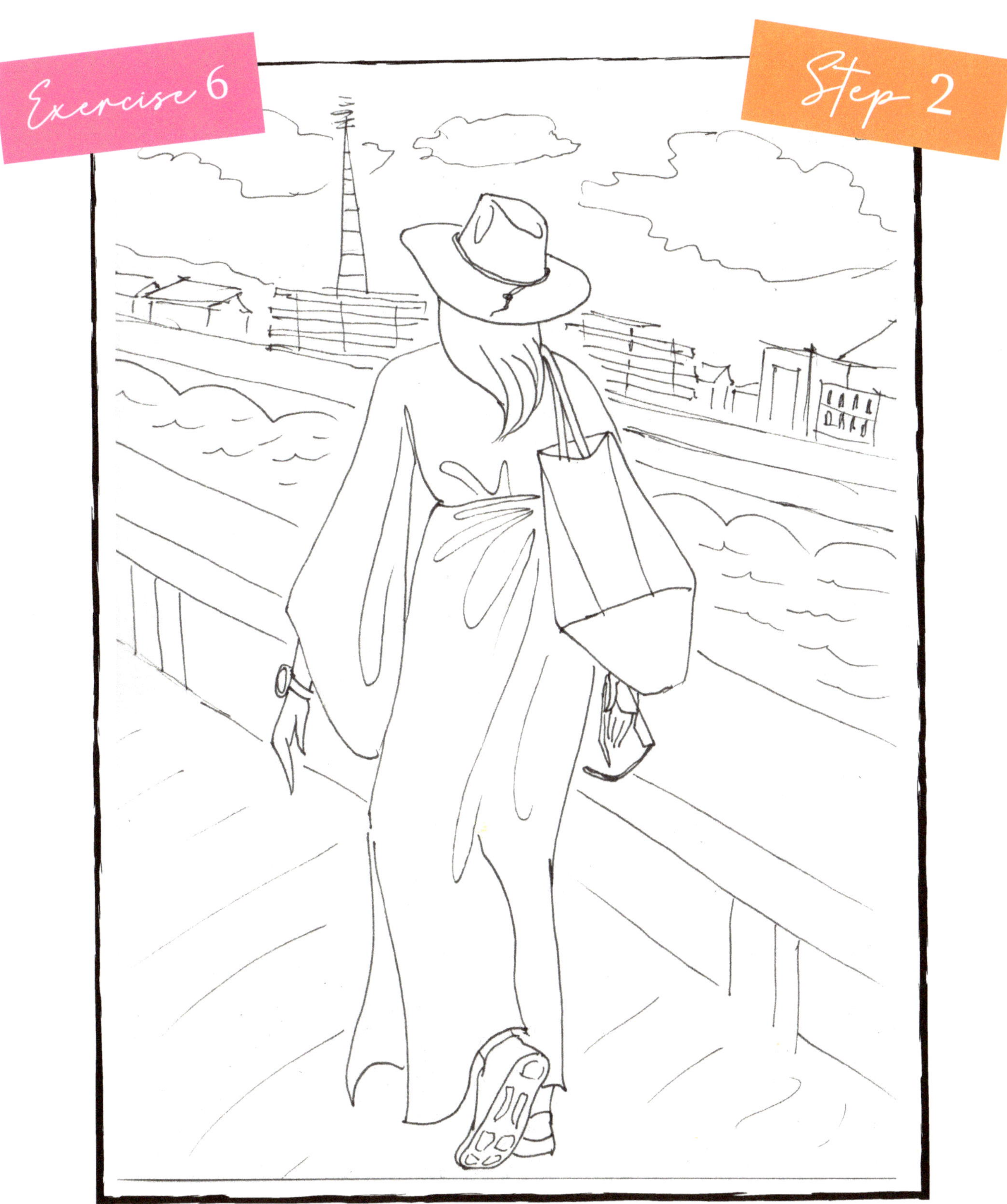

Next, use your pens to outline and add more details to
the sketch. Choose which lines you want to keep and which
ones you will erase. Add waves, building details, accessories,
and other details you wish to emphasize.

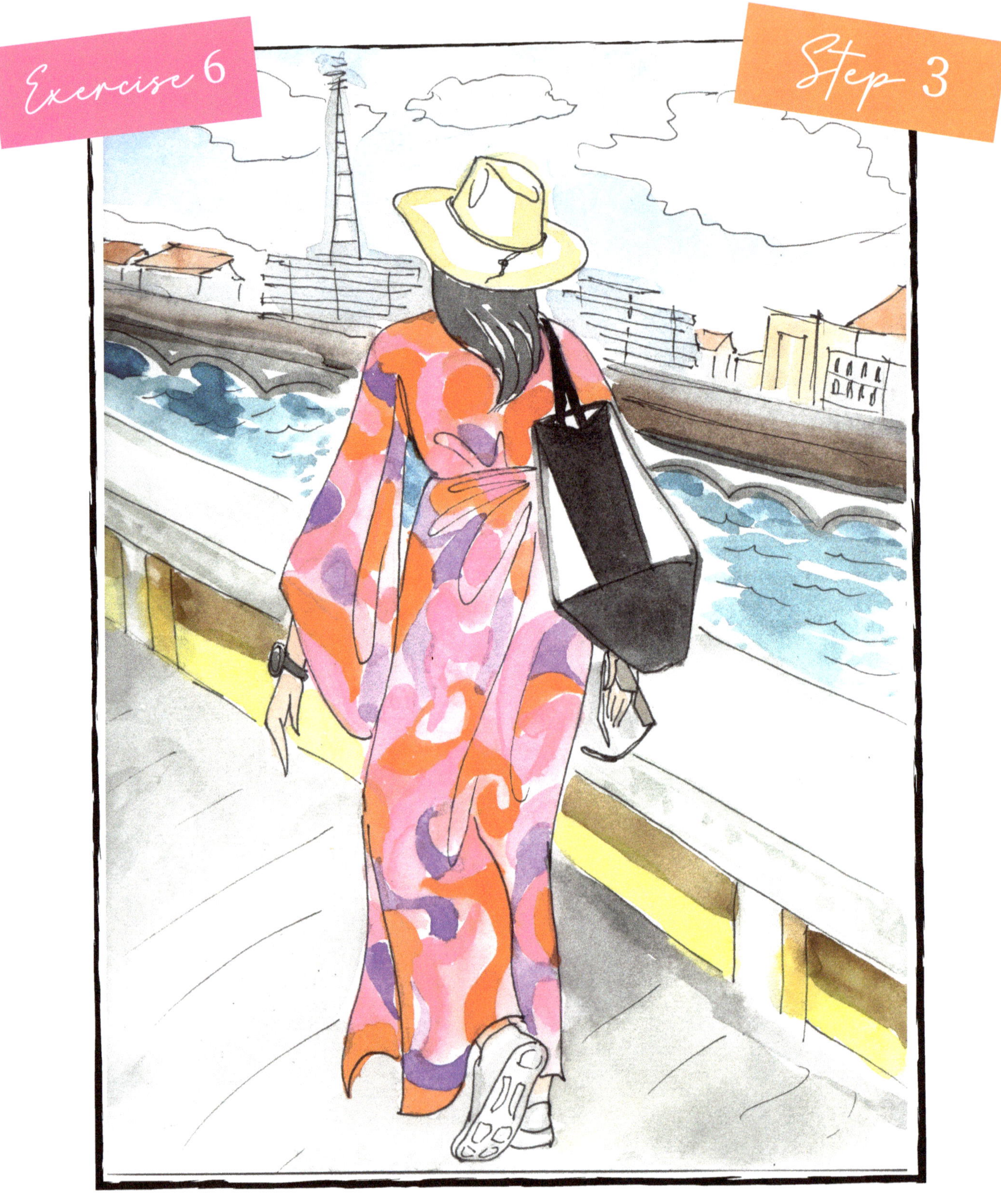

Now let's apply watercolor. Have fun with the colorful print of the cover-up/dress. The pattern doesn't need to be exact, so you can take liberties to enhance and to modify it in any way that you wish.

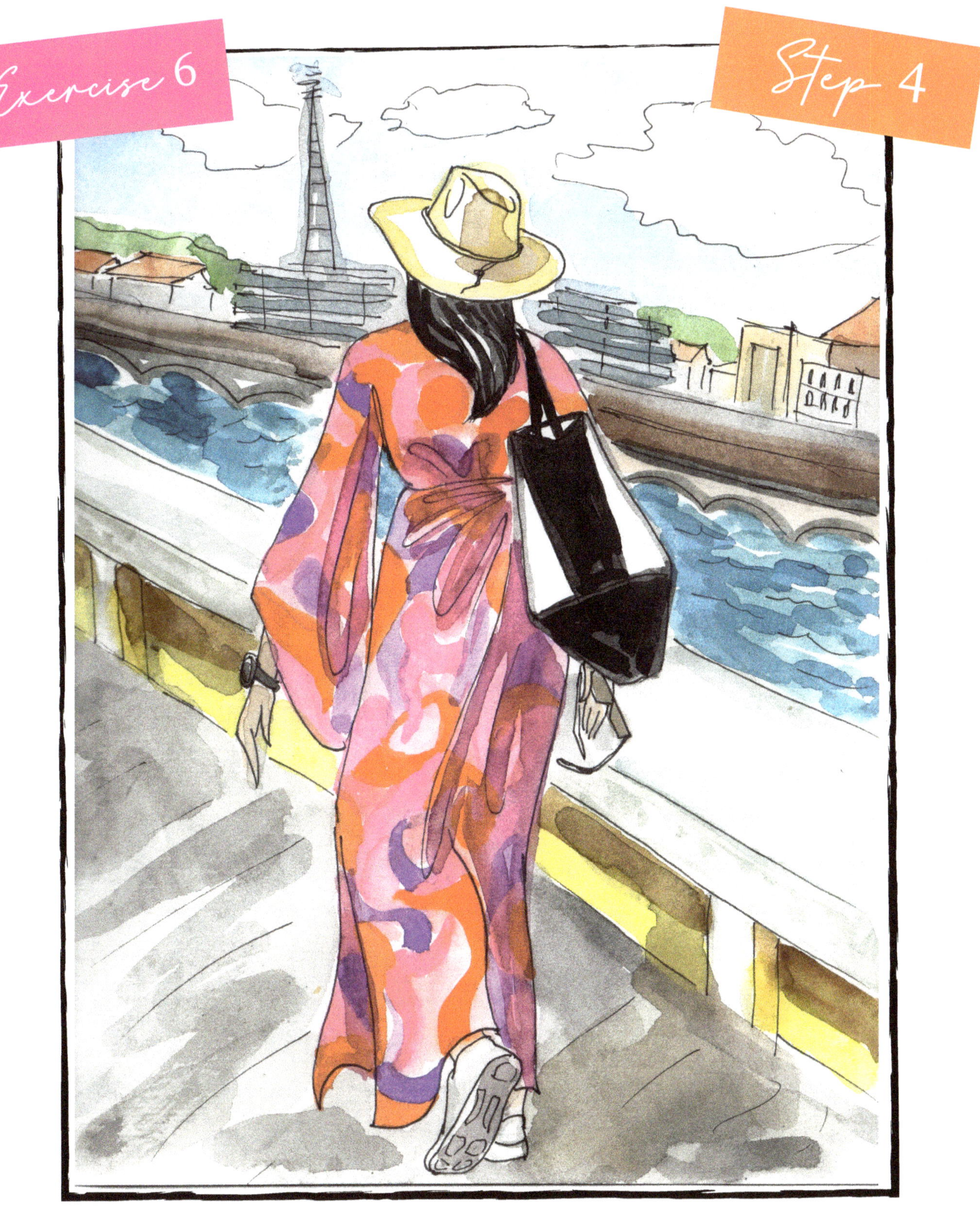

After your first layer of watercolor dries, you can apply the second layer. This time you can emphasize shadows, garment folds, more shades of the water and the road.

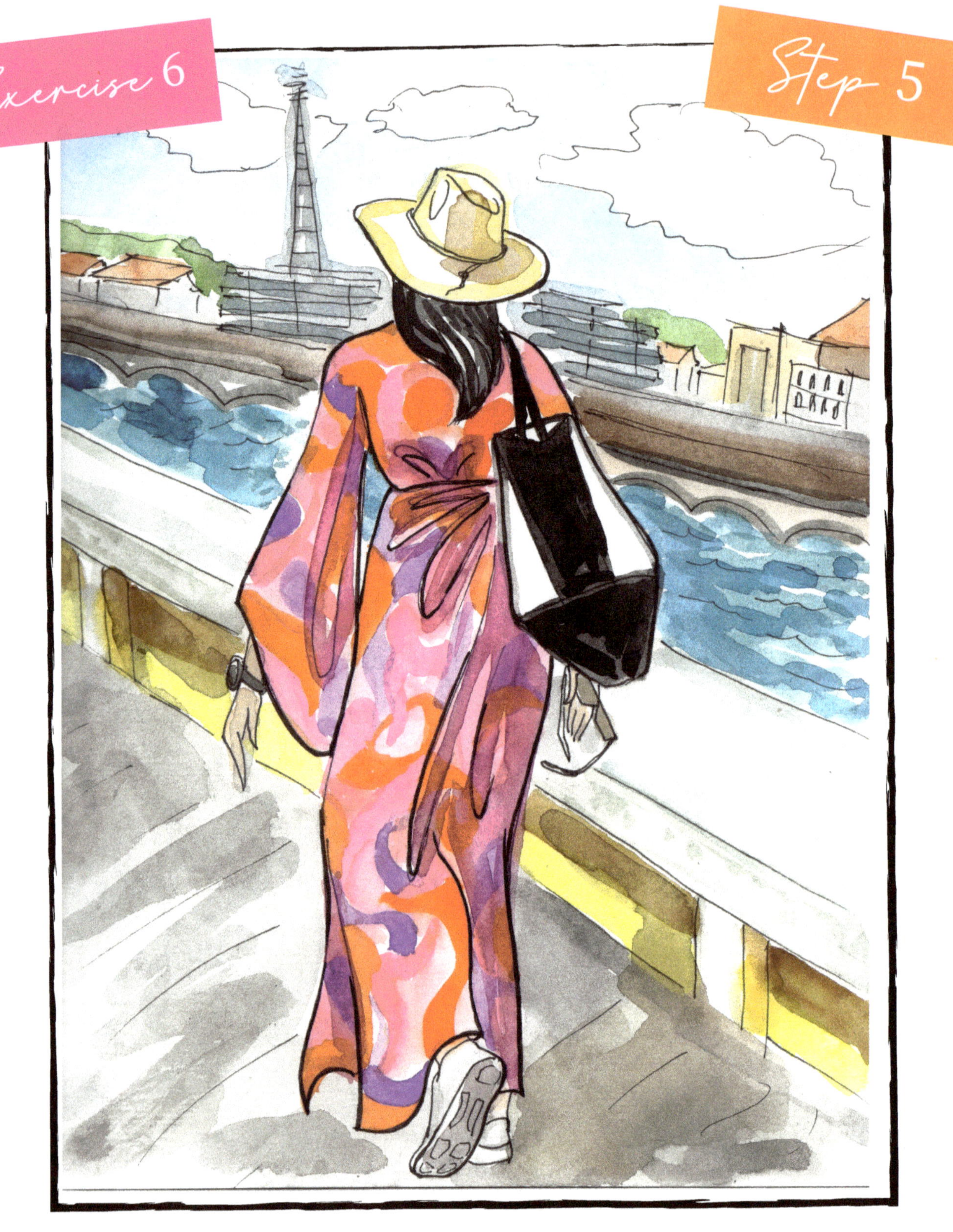

For this particular illustration, I wanted to outline the woman's dress, bag and hat, as a last touch, to make the artwork a bit more polished. This step is optional.

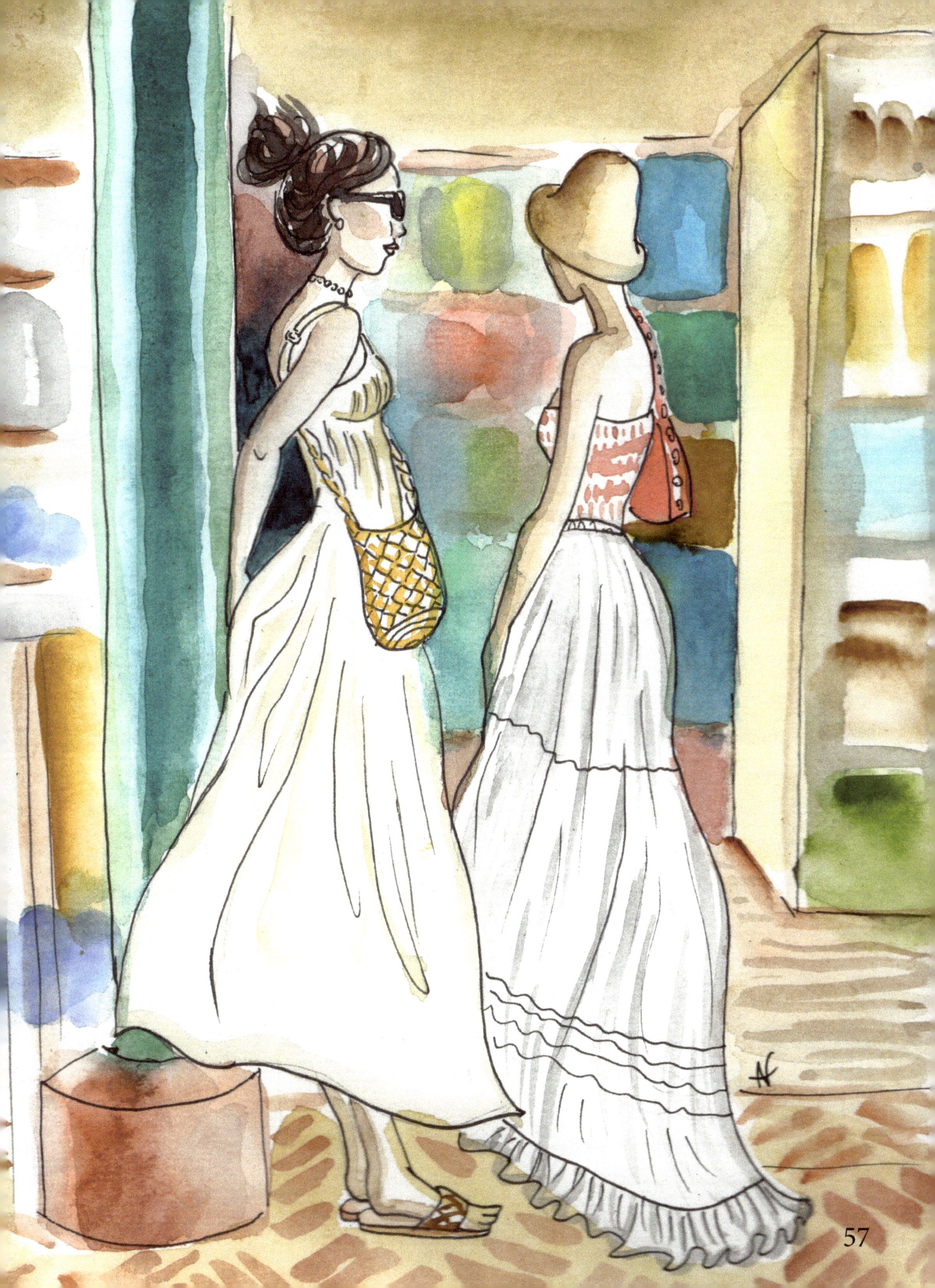

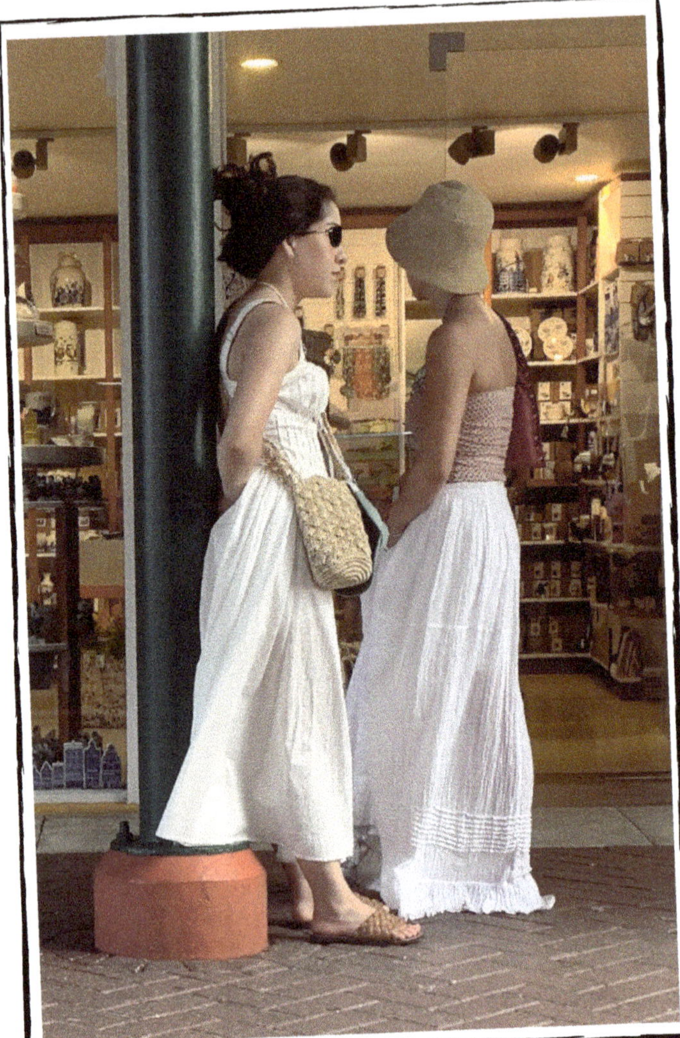

Now let us create a composition from a photo with two models. There is a store seen in the background. As always, the figures are at the center of our composition. Their light colored clothing stands out against the colorful background.
It's a fun way to play with color and value.

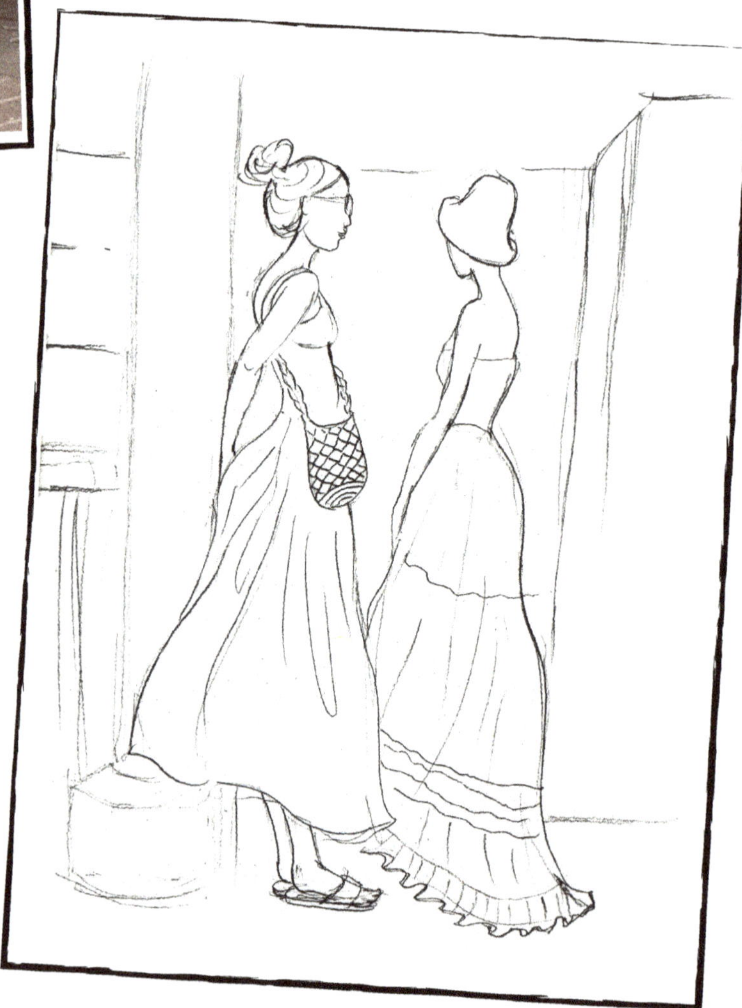

When you sketch the figures, make sure they fit well within the composition, with some room above their heads and below the feet.

You can simplify the drawing – so it's not necessary to draw out all of the items inside the store.

The figures here overlap in an interesting way, thus creating an engaging composition.

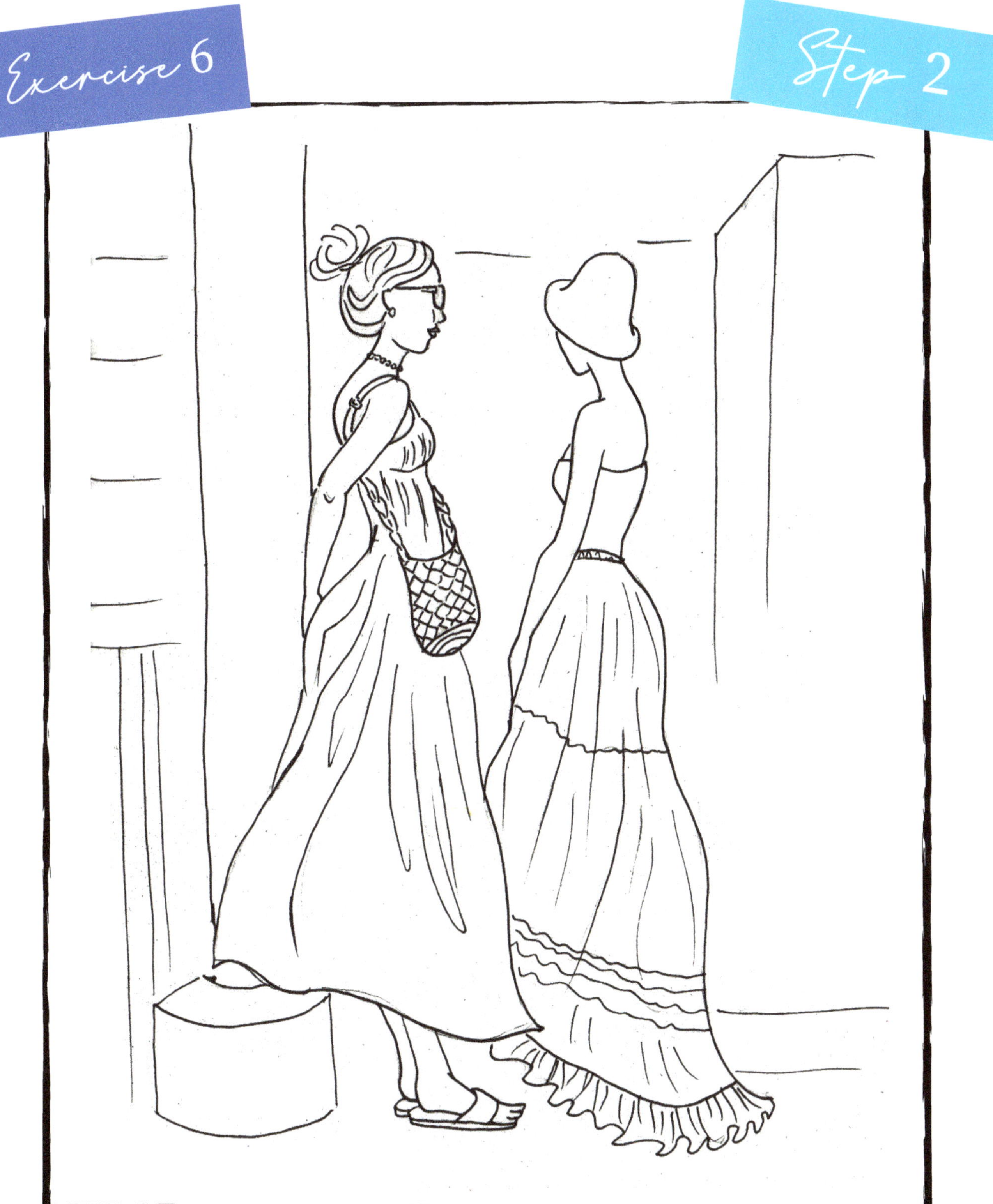

The next step is optional, but if you would like to make your
drawing sharper, you can always outline it with artist pens.
Erase the extra pencil lines after you are done. At this step,
it is still not necessary to draw out your store shelves and items.

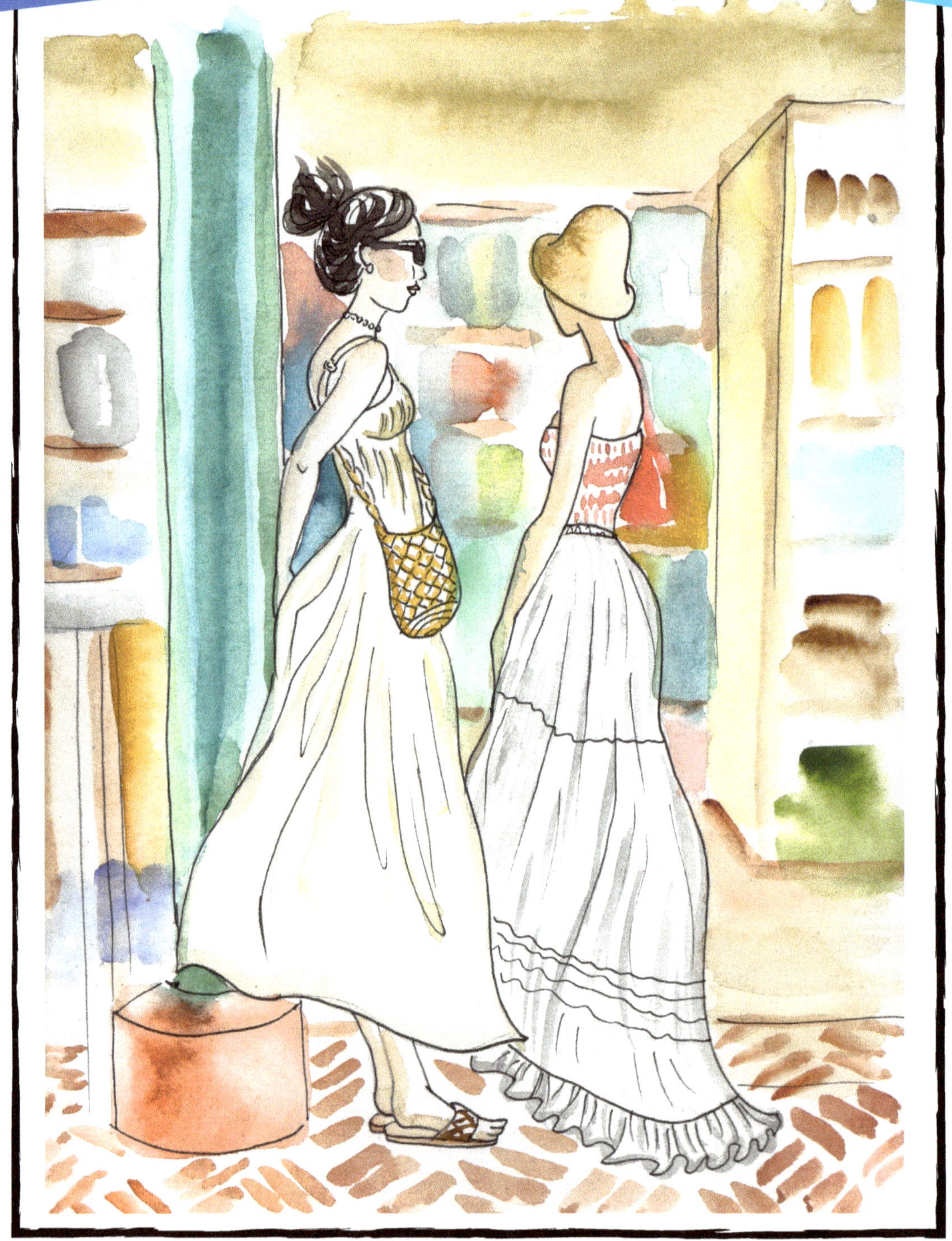

Now let's apply the first layer of watercolor. Note the way I indicated the store items and shelves here – similar to a photo with a backdrop that is out of focus. This way, all attention is on the fashion figures in the front. Remember to keep a lot of the white of the paper for the ladies' garments.

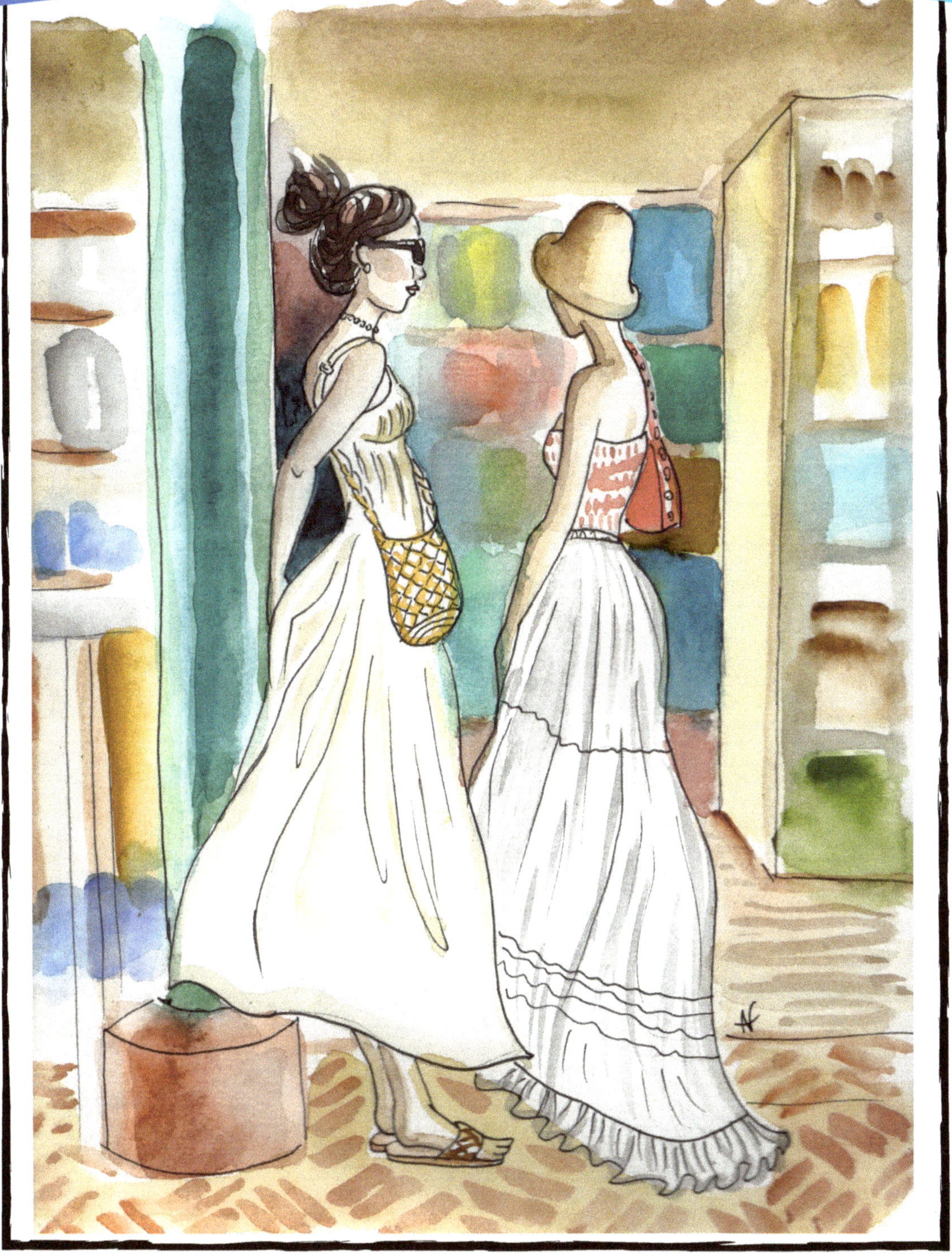

Finally, once our first watercolor layer has dried, we can apply shading and more color layers to our illustration. Don't over-work the painting, keep it fresh. Add more deep colors around the ladies in light clothing, to emphasize the contrast.

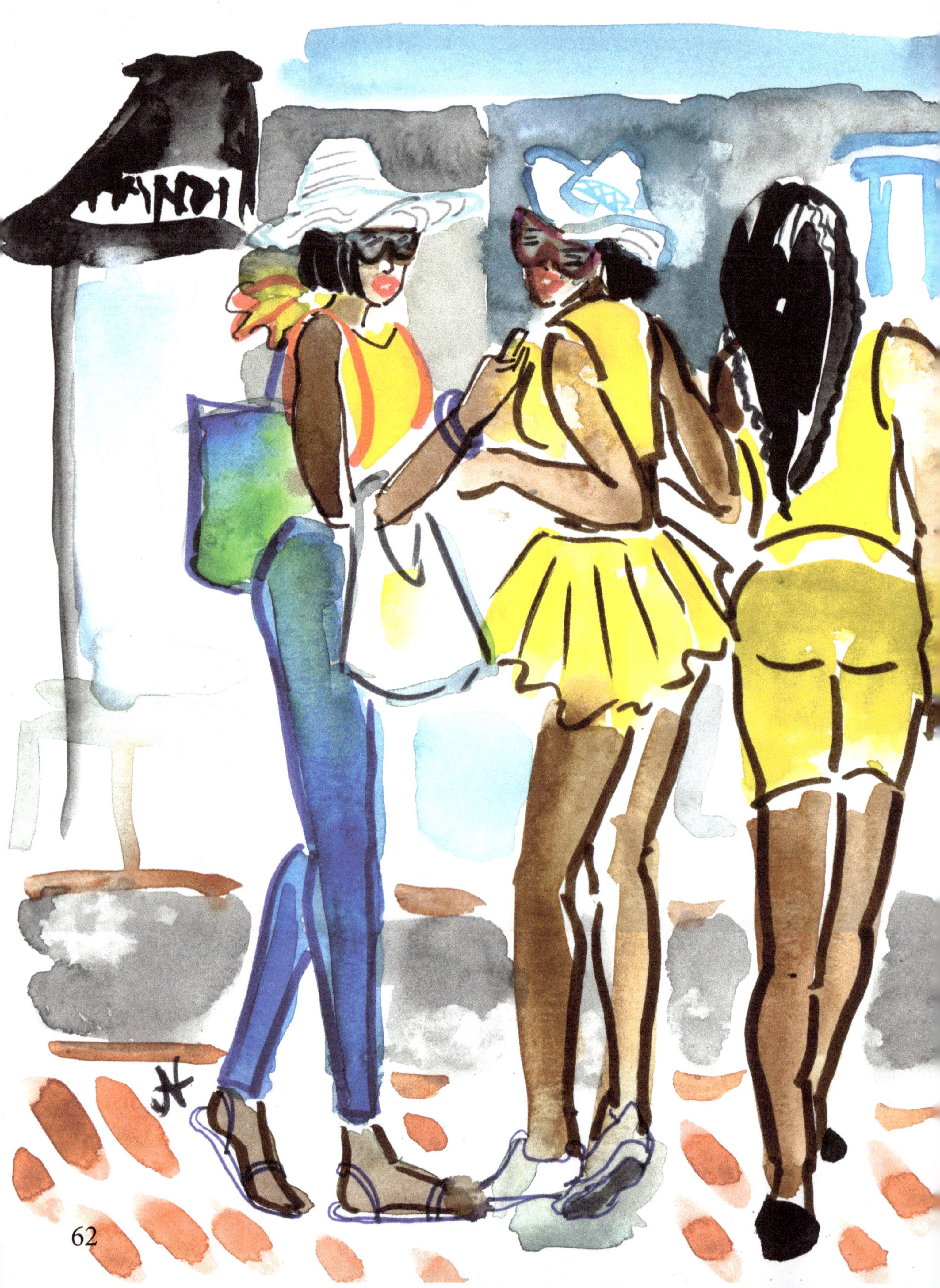

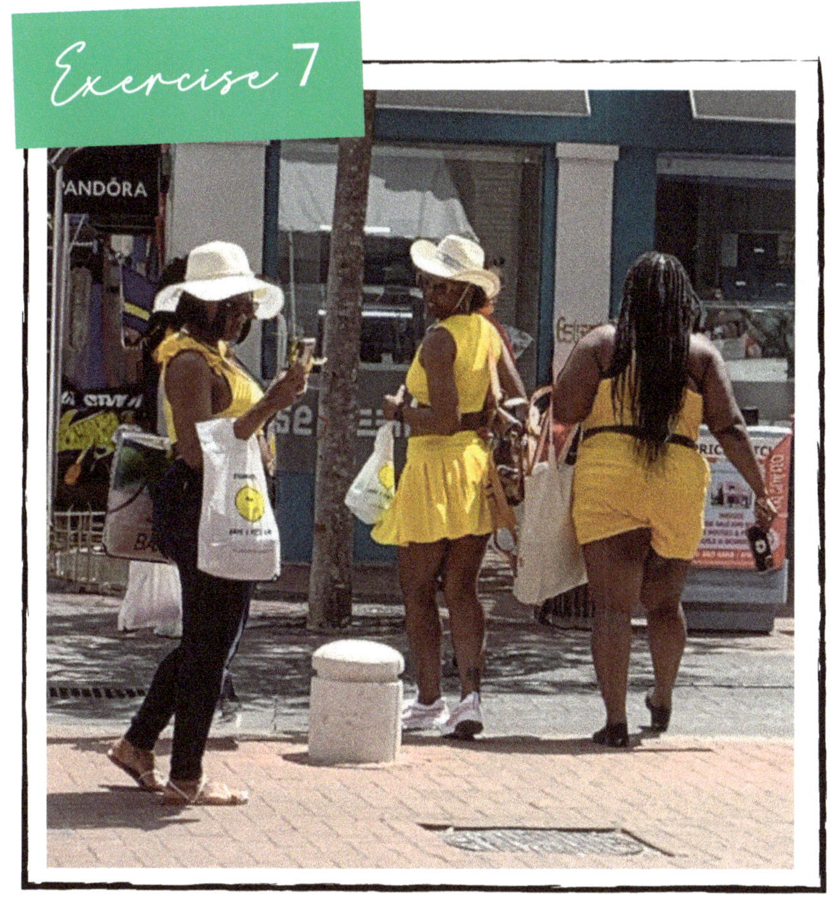

Finally, our last painting from a photo in this book will feature a composition with three ladies.
When I saw these ladies, I thought they would be perfect models for this book. They were all wearing yellow outfits and looked fabulous in the scene.
For this exercise, let's do straight watercolor, similar to the art exercise at beginning of the book.

Once you develop some skills, you can draw from a photo directly with your watercolors. First, paint the three figures in yellow. Use dynamic lines. Keep their heads small to leave enough room for the rest of their bodies.

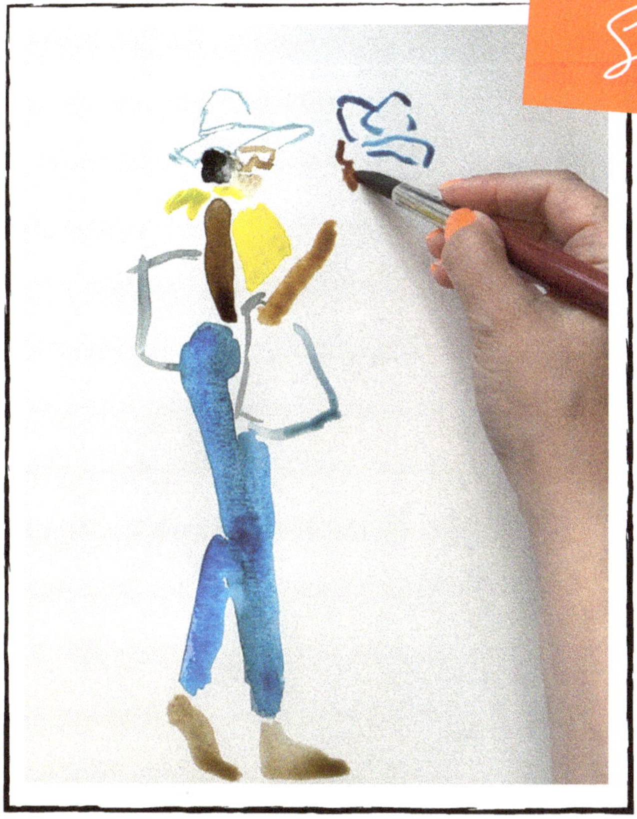

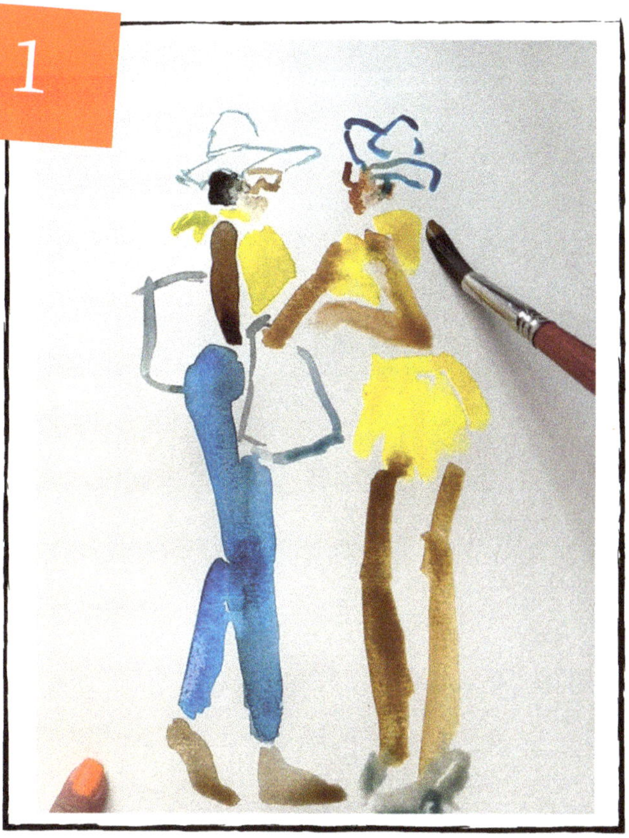

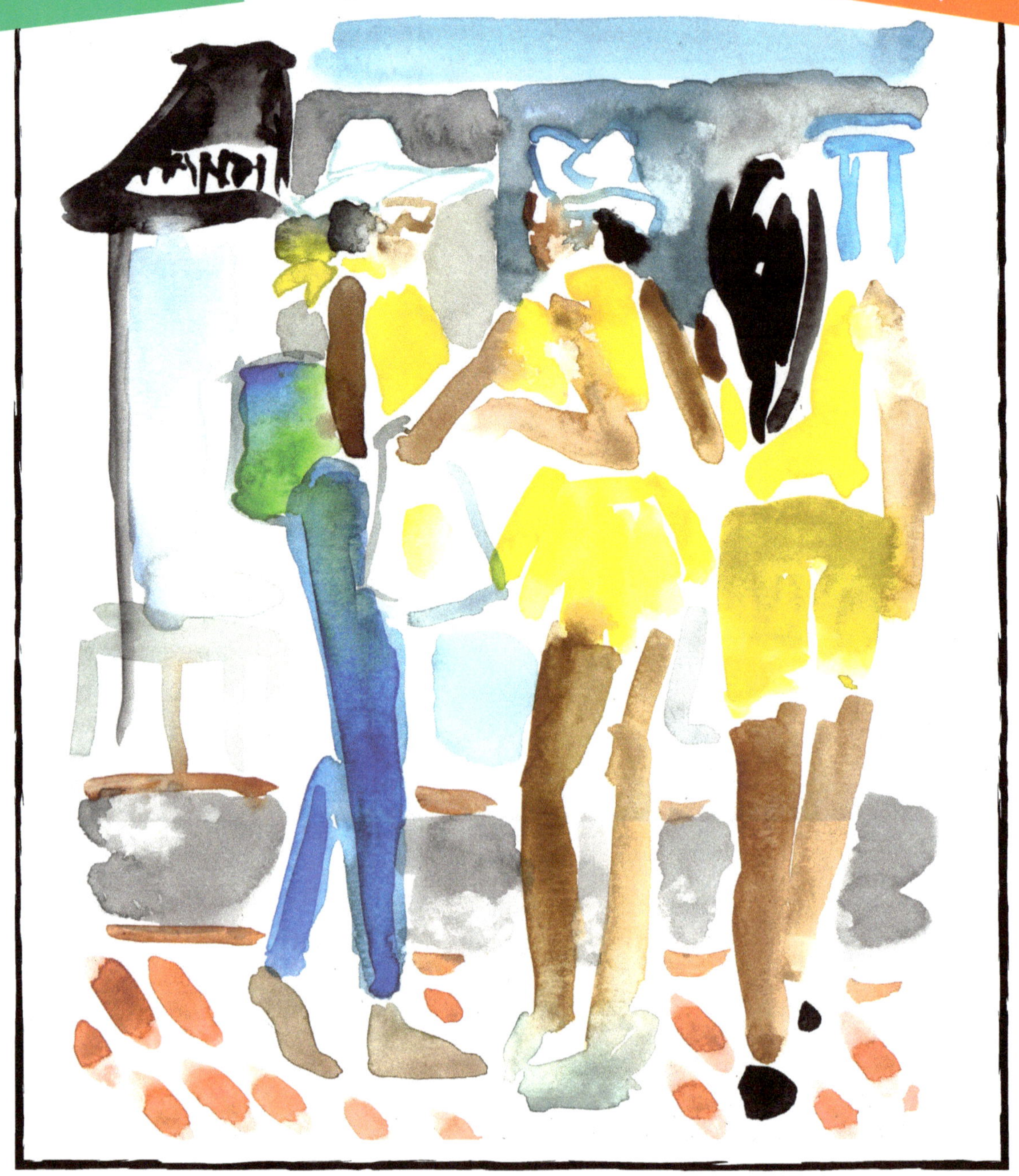

Once you paint your loose fashion illustration of the three ladies in yellow, you can then paint the background. Keep it loose, free, expressive, and without too many details. Once the first layer of watercolor dries, apply a second layer, to deepen colors of the background and/or the women and clothes.

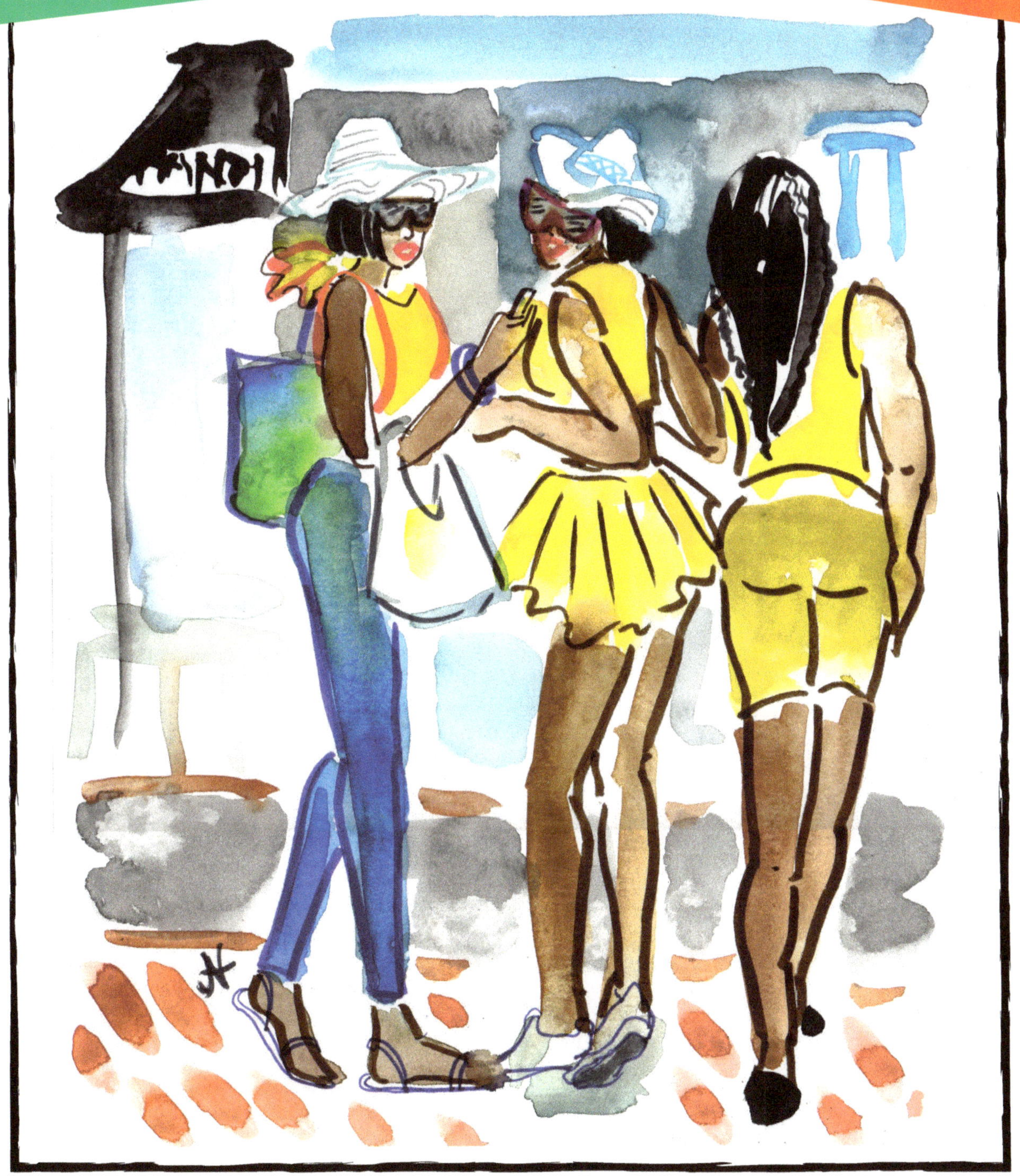

Finally, when everything dries, you can add outlines in brush markers on the figures. Note that I added details in their clothes, shoes, hair, and accessories. This pulls our drawing together, to make it more polished and finished.

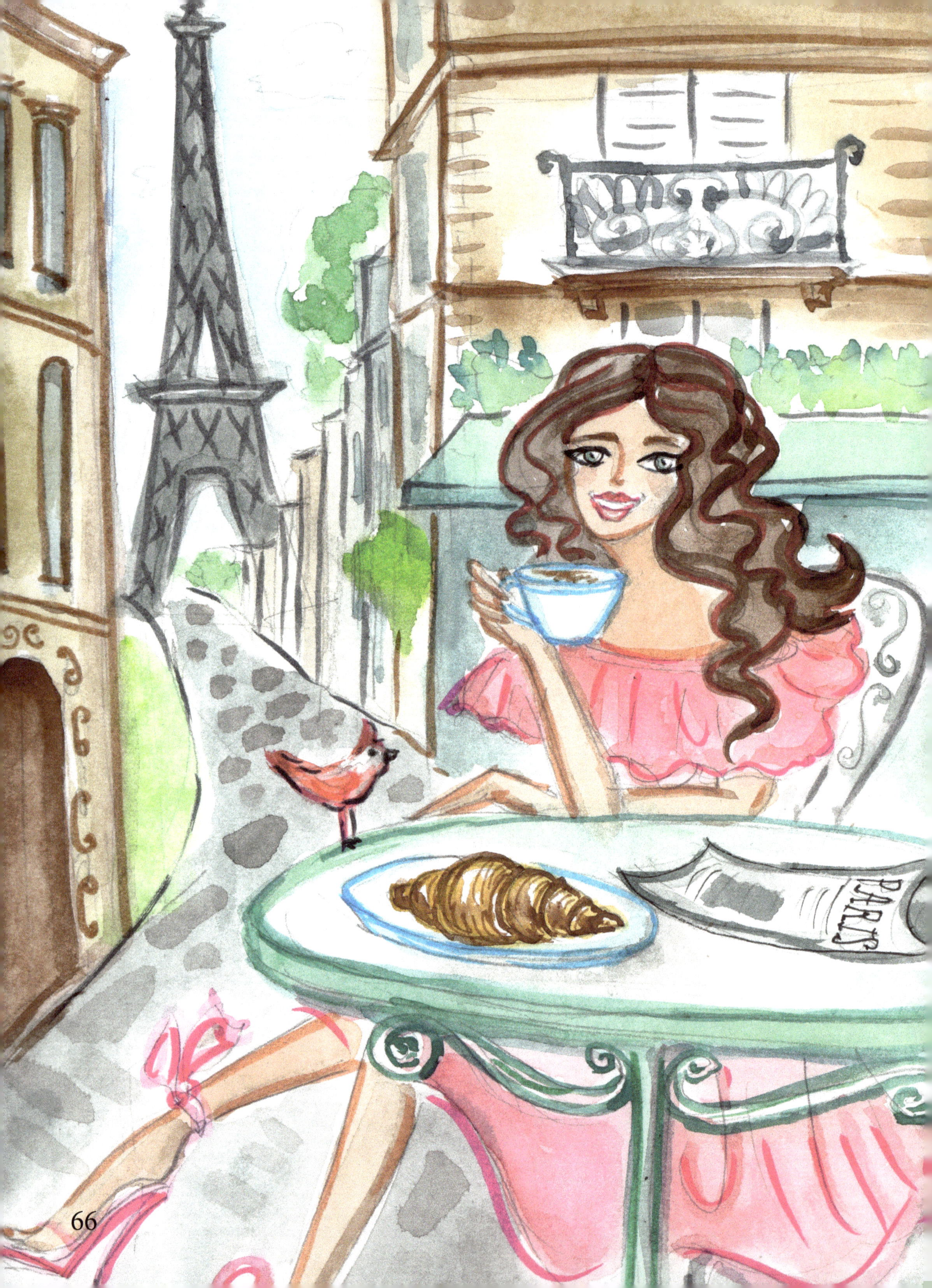

PARIS

Now that we have explored creating fashion compositions from photos, let's dive into coming up with our own ideas for fashion compositions. You can combine your own travel references, photos found online, fun art ideas from your research. Here I have created my own "Paris Girl."

This is an example of what you can create when you merge photo references and imagination. This way your art will be completely unique. You can have your character do whatever you want her to do. I wanted my fashion girl to be seated in a cute outdoor French cafe, while she is sipping coffee. She has a croissant on her plate. We can see a cobble stone street and the Eiffel Tower in the background, as well as some buildings.

As always, you can start with a pencil sketch, to get down your ideas.

You can emphasize the details on the old building, such as a wrought iron balcony with intricate designs. Such details will convey the feeling of the scene.

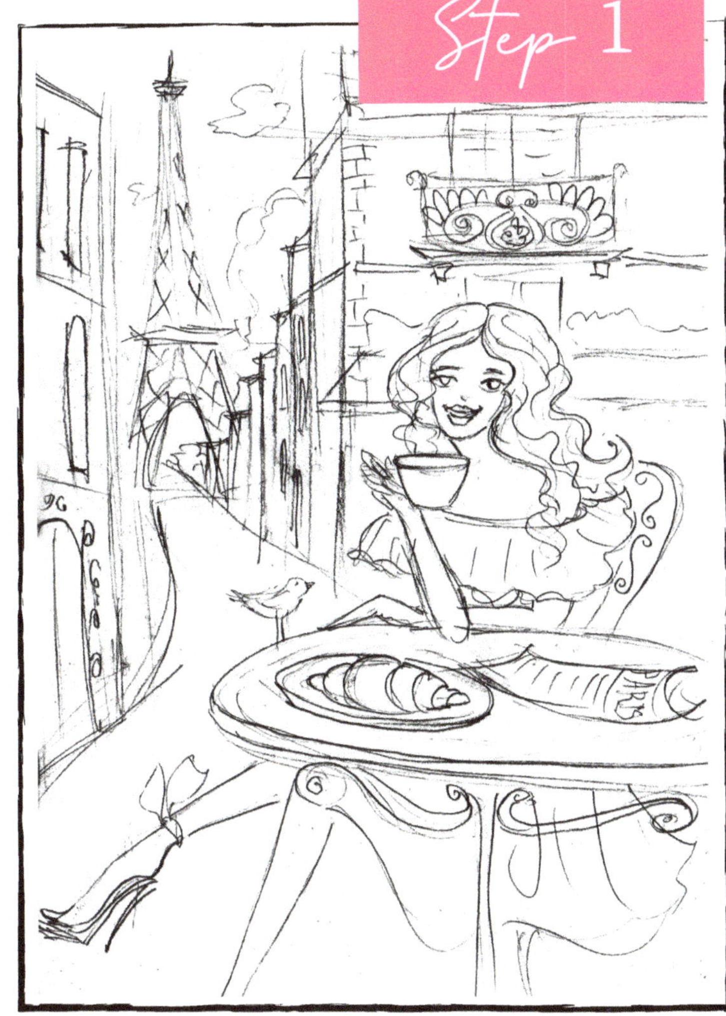

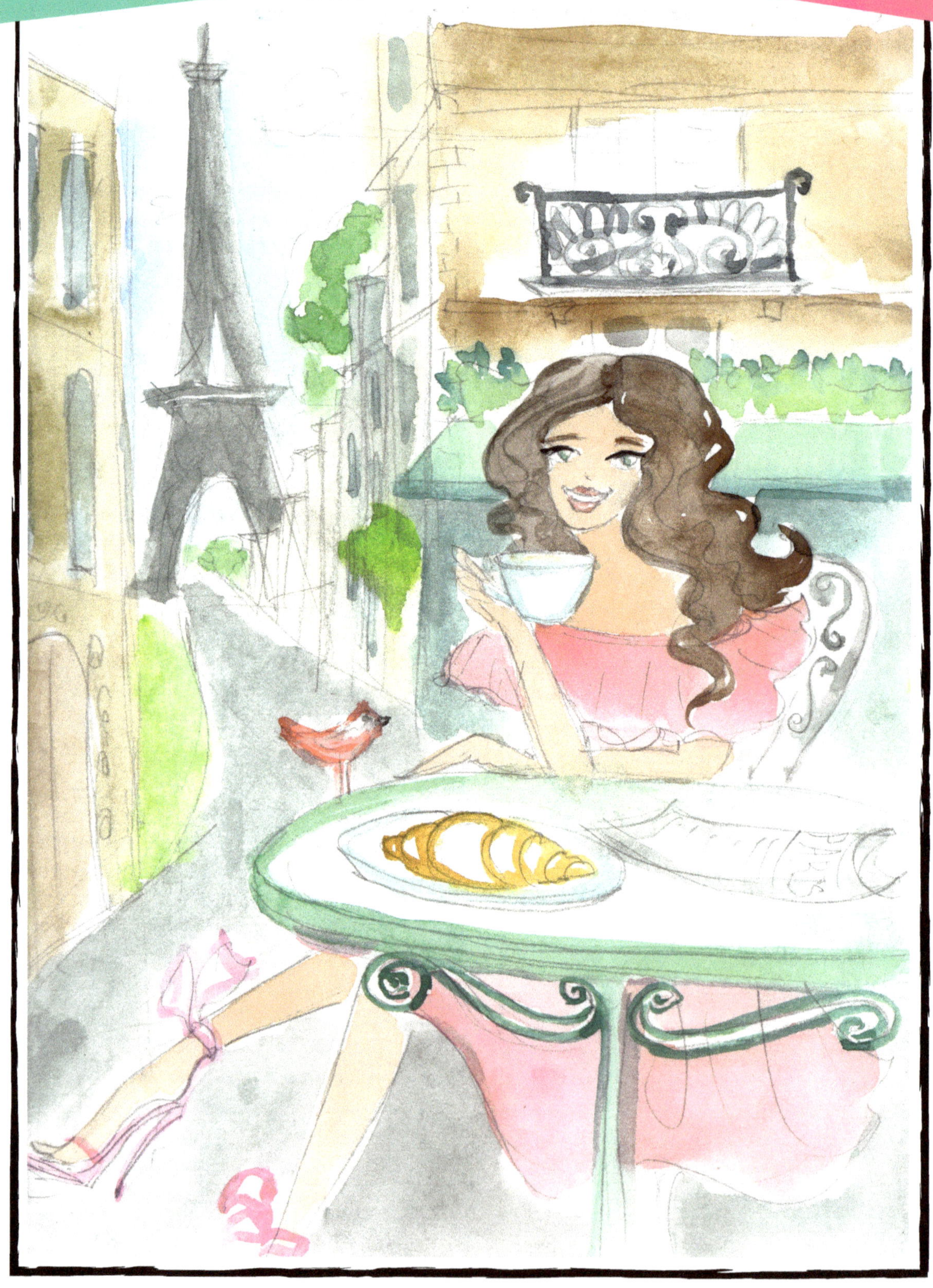

Let's now do a light watercolor wash. You can erase the extra pencil lines before painting and/or after the watercolor dries.

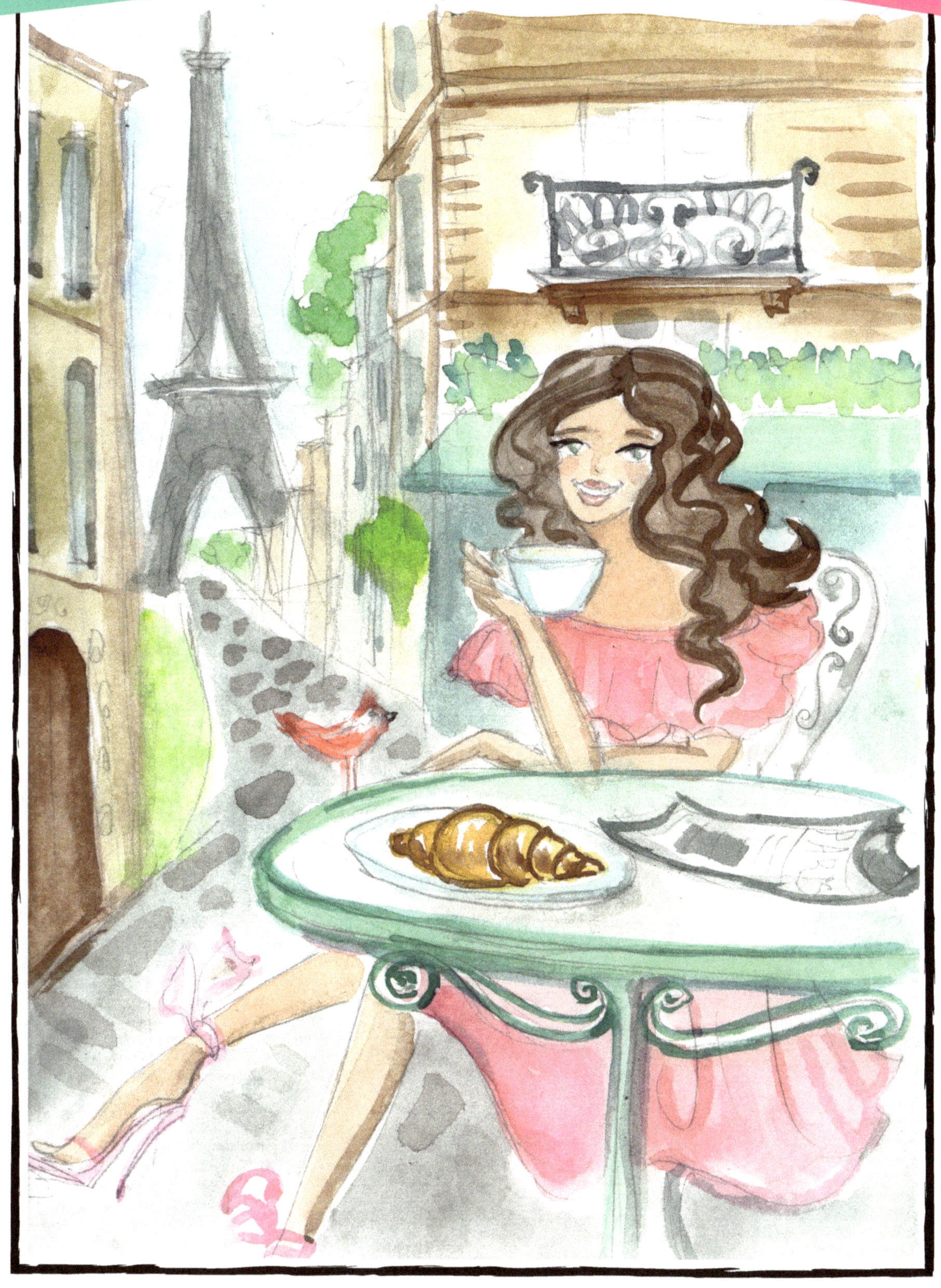

After the first layer dries, add more details and shading with the second watercolor layer.

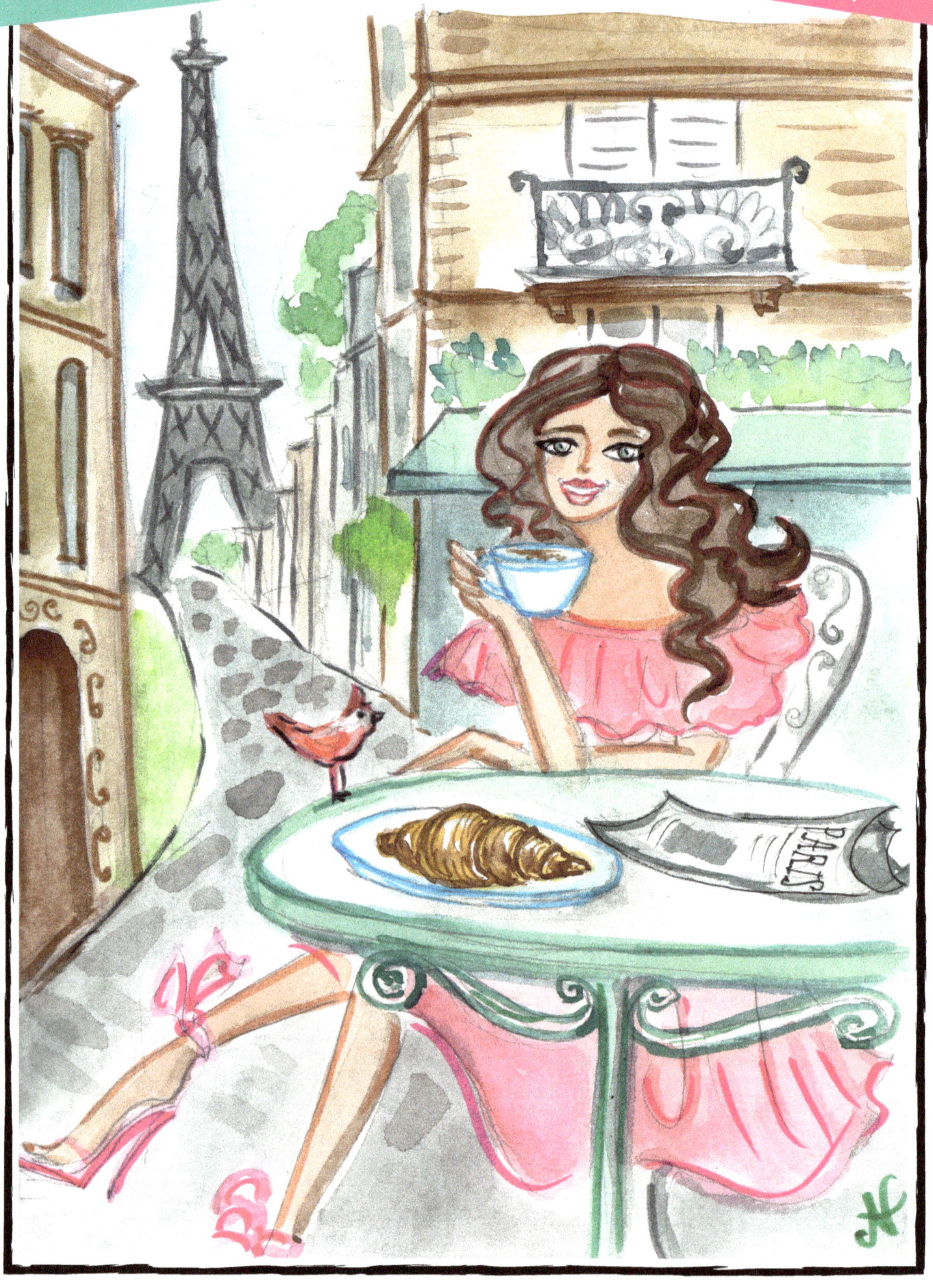

When that dries, we can add accents and details with brush markers. Pay attention to hair, clothing folds, building details, etc.

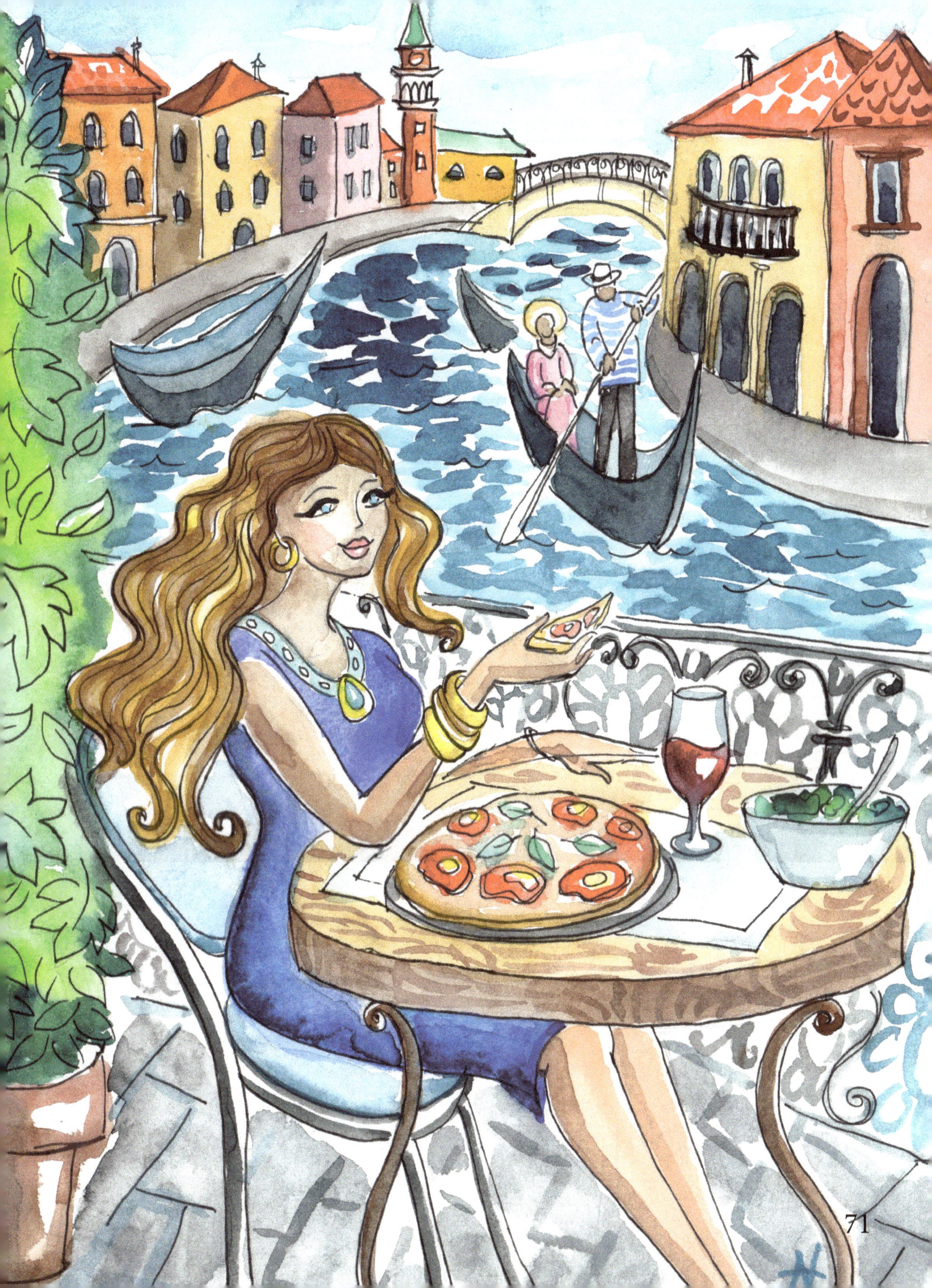

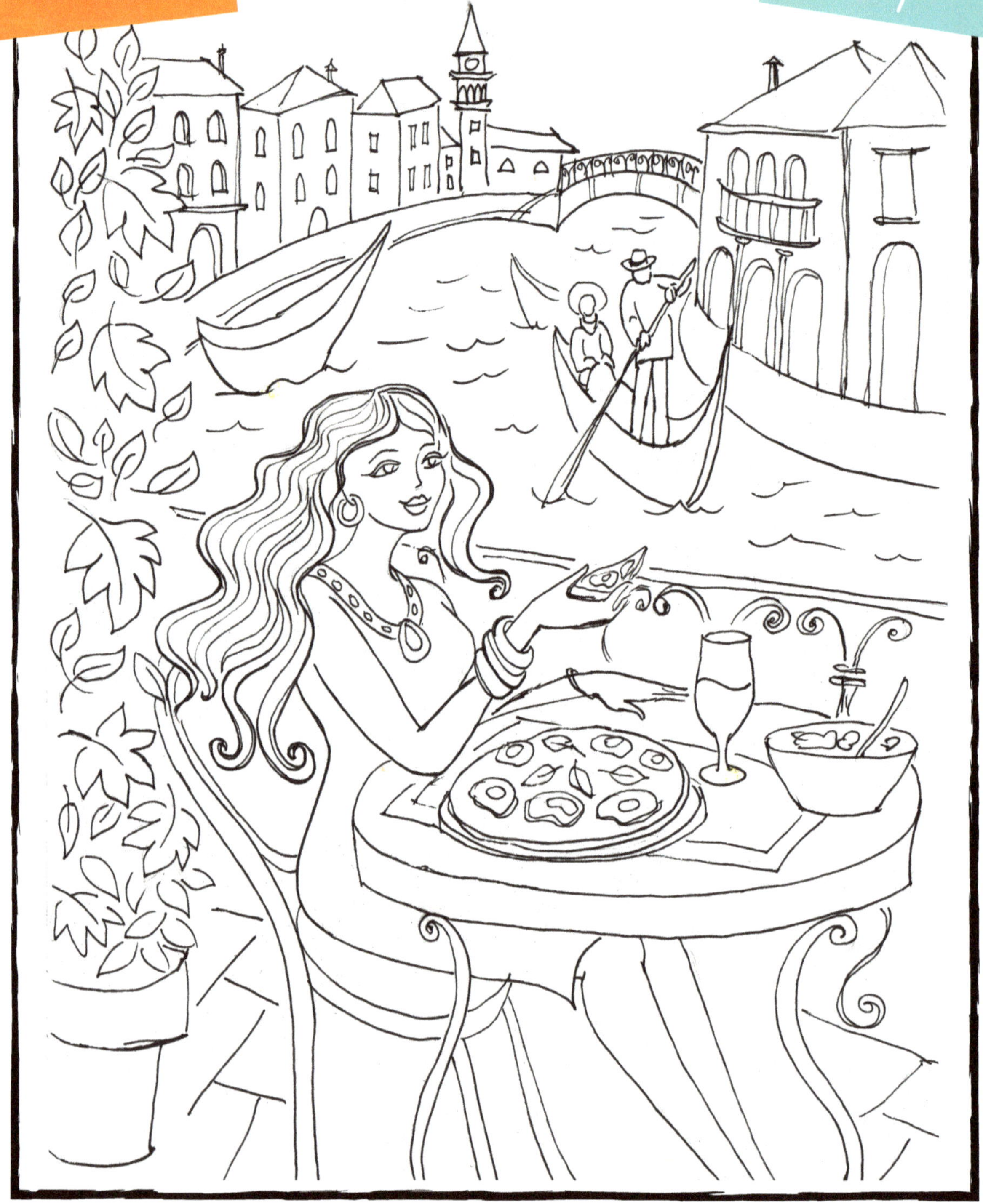

Now let's do a similar exercise with "Venice Girl." I've used photos of Venice I found on-line, combined with some restaurant and plant images, in addition to imagination. You can use this image as a reference to copy and add your own flare to it. After sketching the drawing, I outlined it with artist pens.

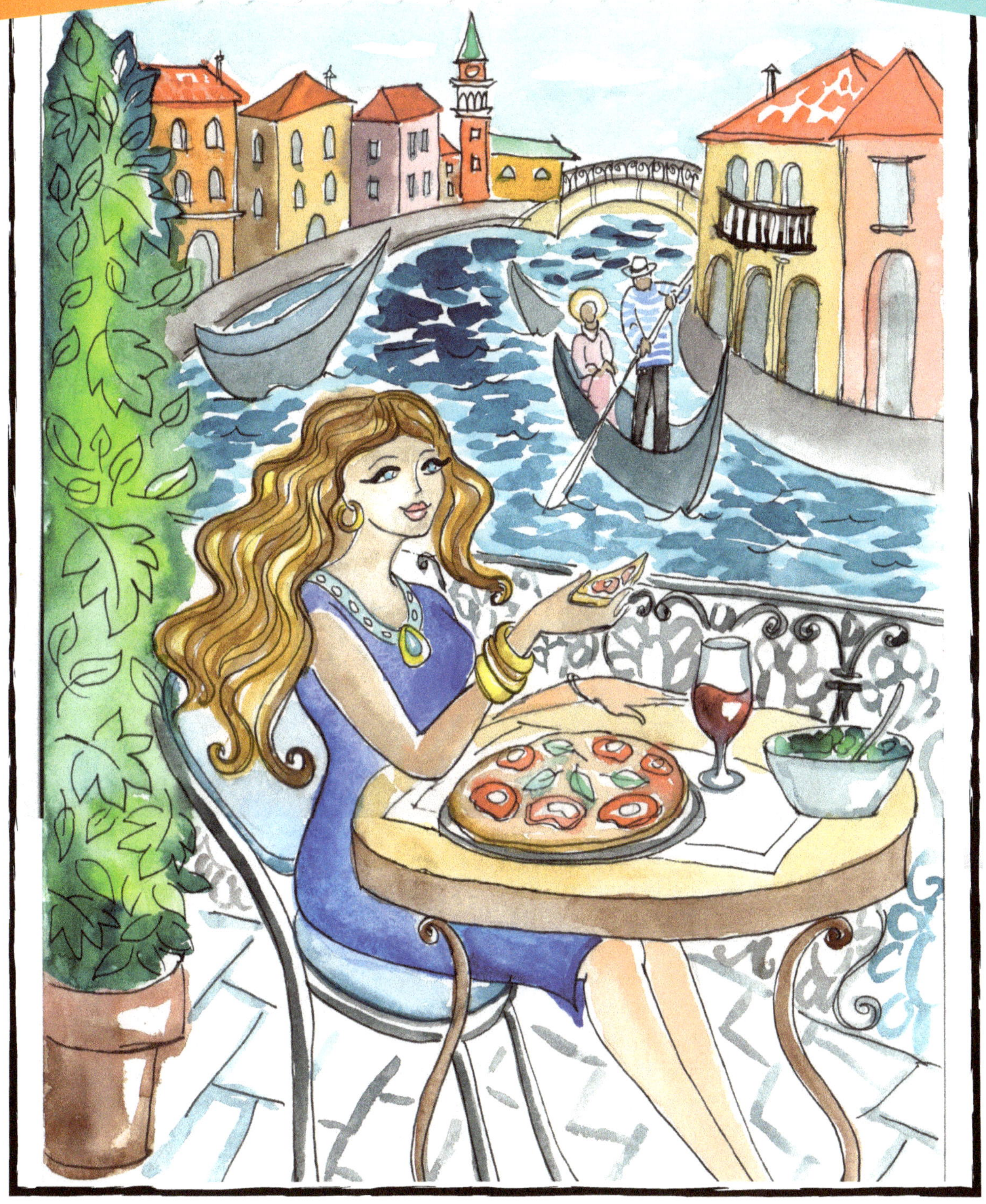

The next step is applying the first layer of watercolor. Let colors run into each other where applicable, like leaves, water, sky, dress, and hair. Dab off extra water where you don't wish the colors to run.

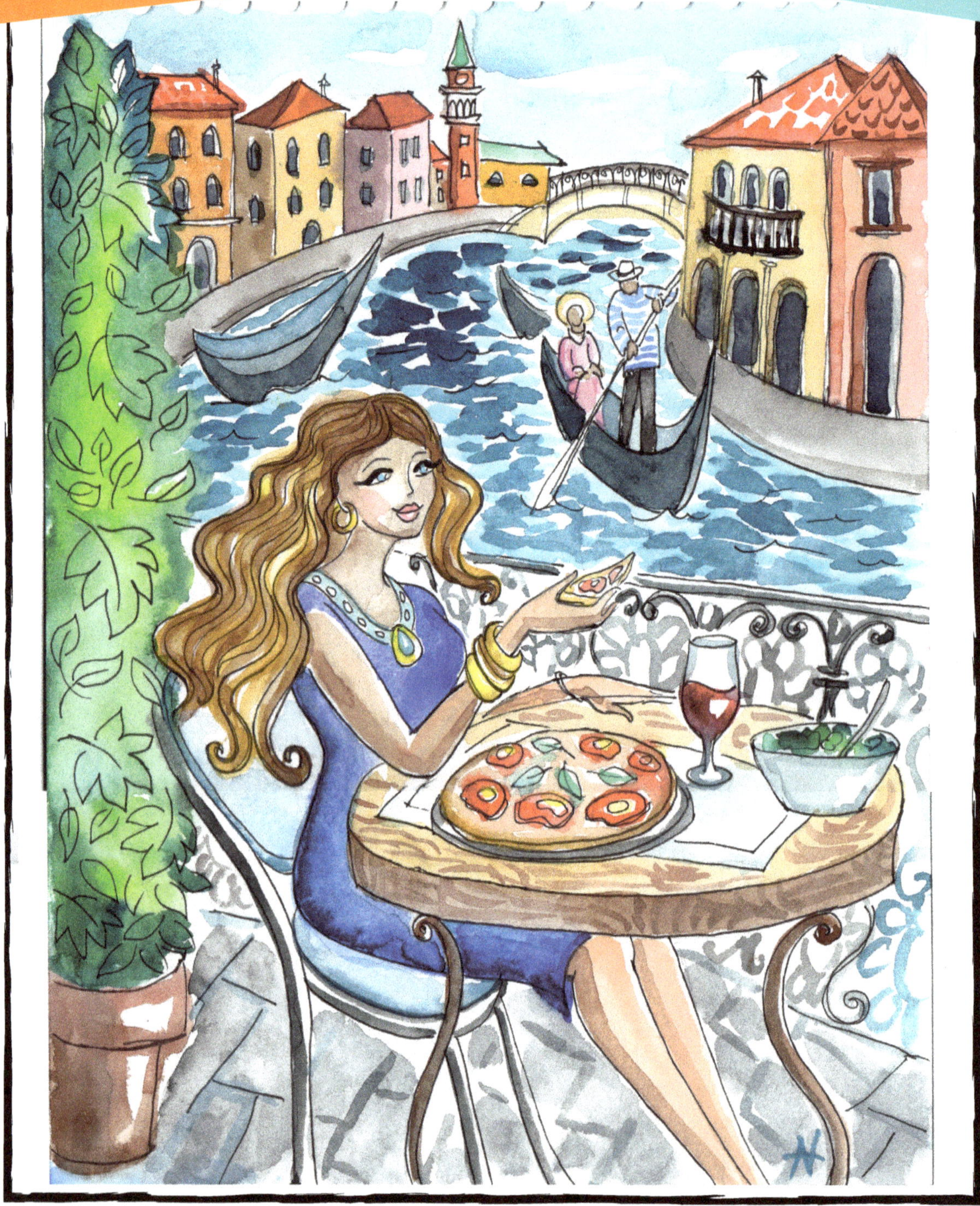

Finally, add shading with the next watercolor layer. Add more details as well. Now your art looks more finished and the colors are more saturated. Feel free to add your own details wherever you see fit.

A great way to improve your figure and scene drawing sills and to keep them sharp is to practice drawing on location. But you don't have to carry all of your numerous art supplies with you. All you need to create fantastic and quick location sketches is a small watercolor paper pad and a tiny travel watercolor paint set, plus several pens/markers.

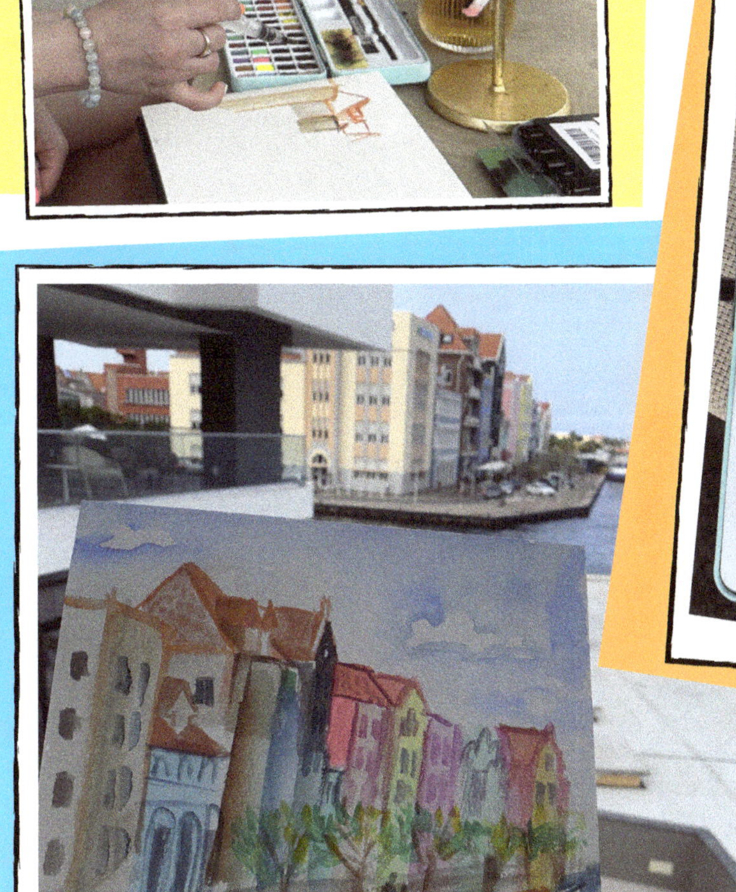

You can find many ready to use watercolor travel sets on sites such as Amazon, and art supply stores.

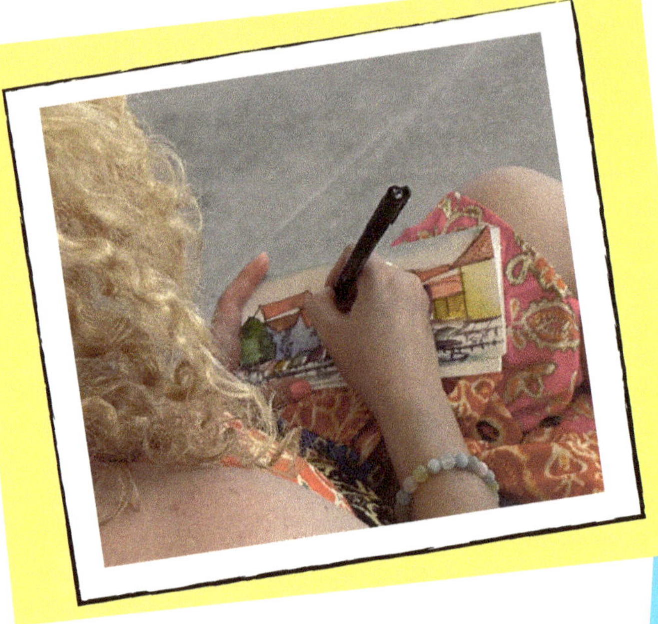

First, find an interesting subject you would like to capture in your sketch. Here is a view of an outdoor market and colorful buildings.

Then find a good spot to sit and draw your subject. You want to be comfortable, while getting a good view of the scene.

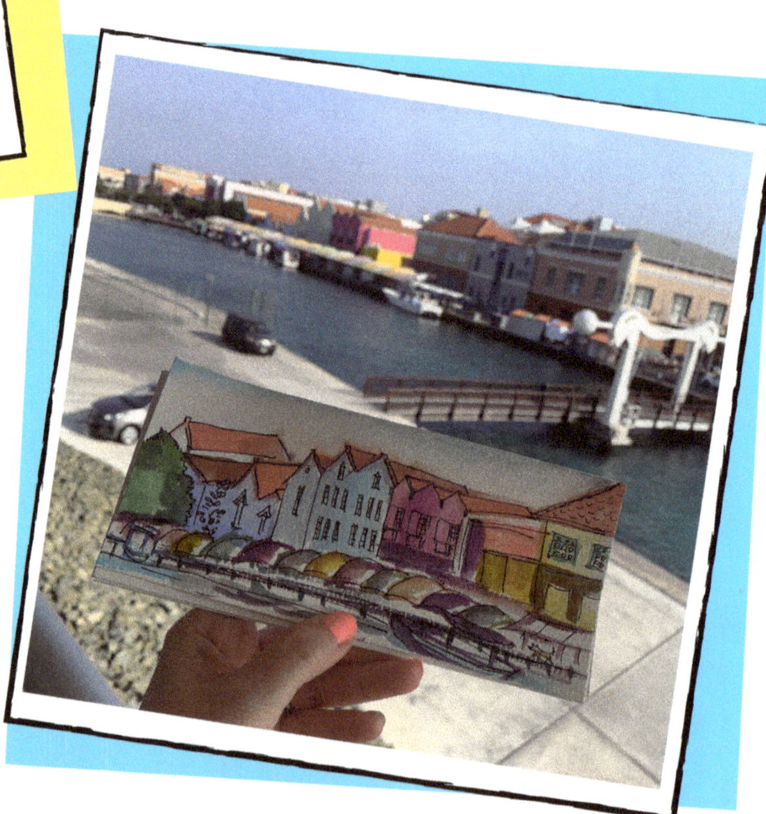

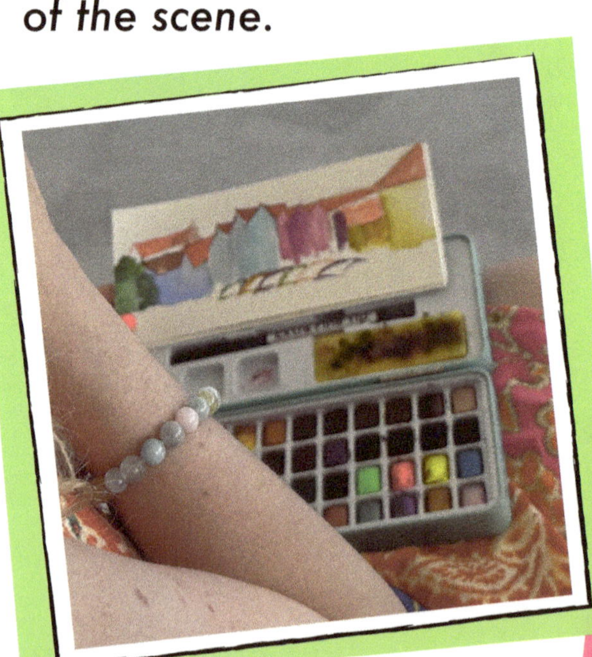

You can either first draw out the scene with pens or markers, or go straight in with your watercolors.

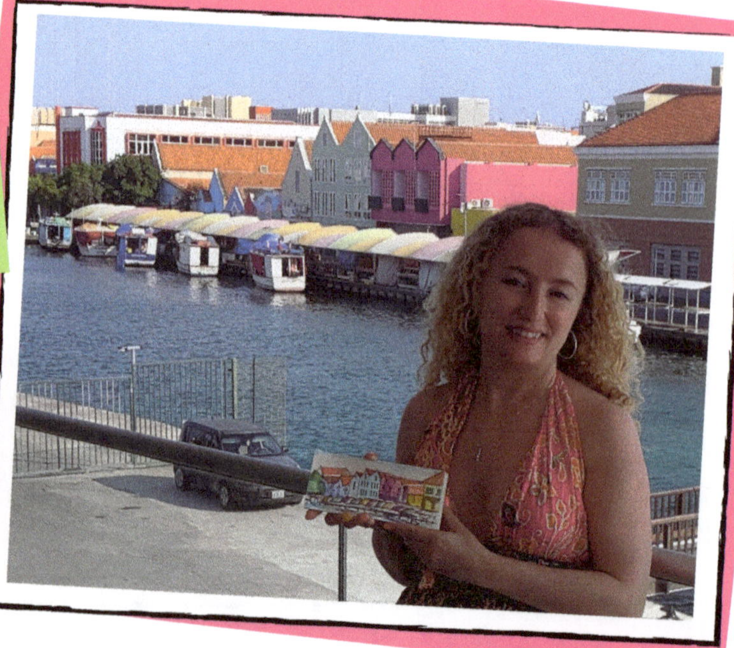

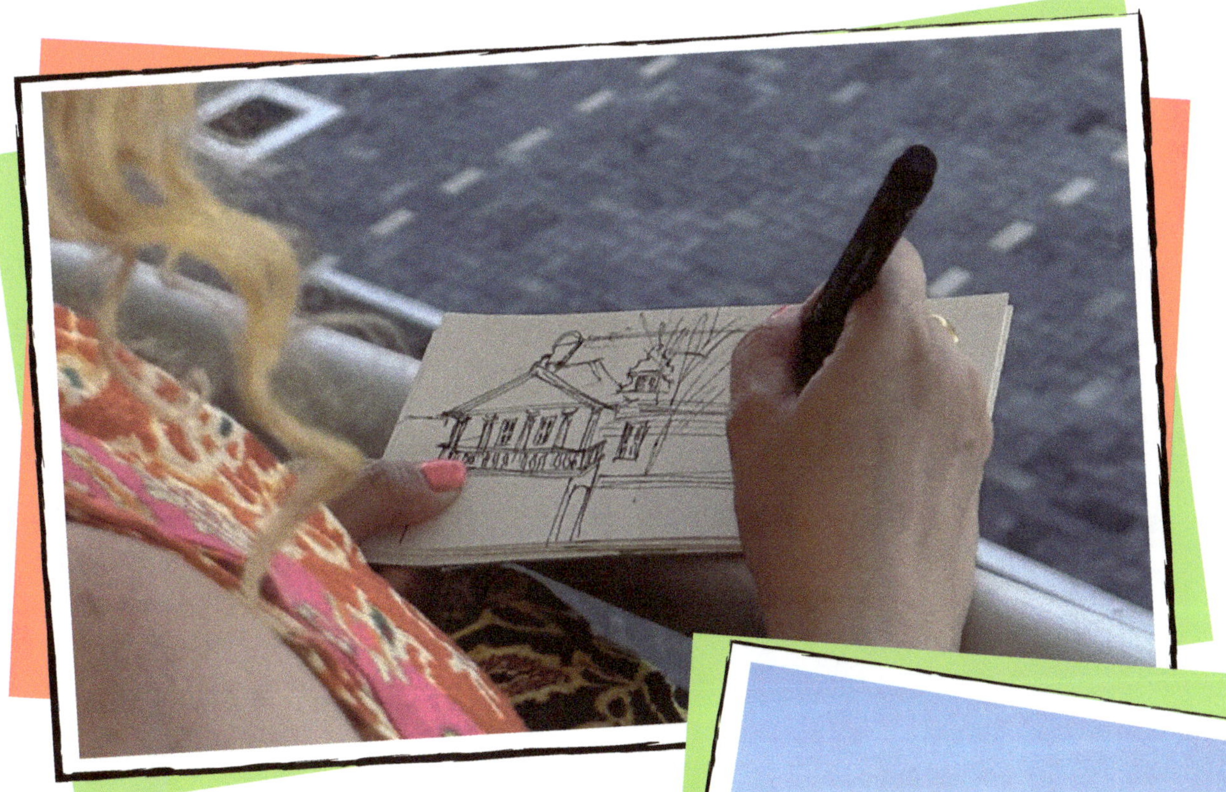

I encourage you to ditch the pencil when you do your location art. When you work directly with pens or watercolors, you are forced to be brave, bold and to develop problem solving skills.

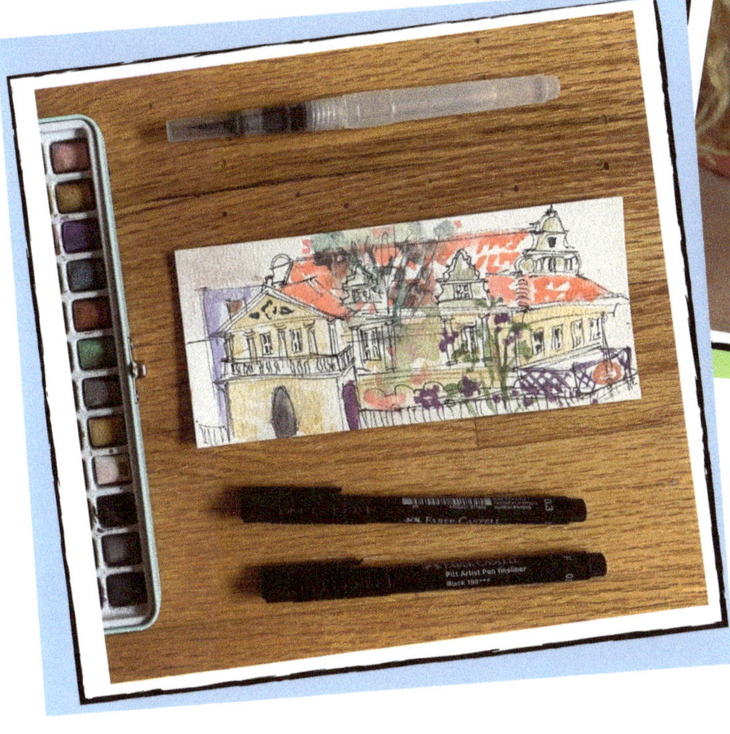

Your lines will eventually become more confident, and you will learn to be more discerning when you draw.

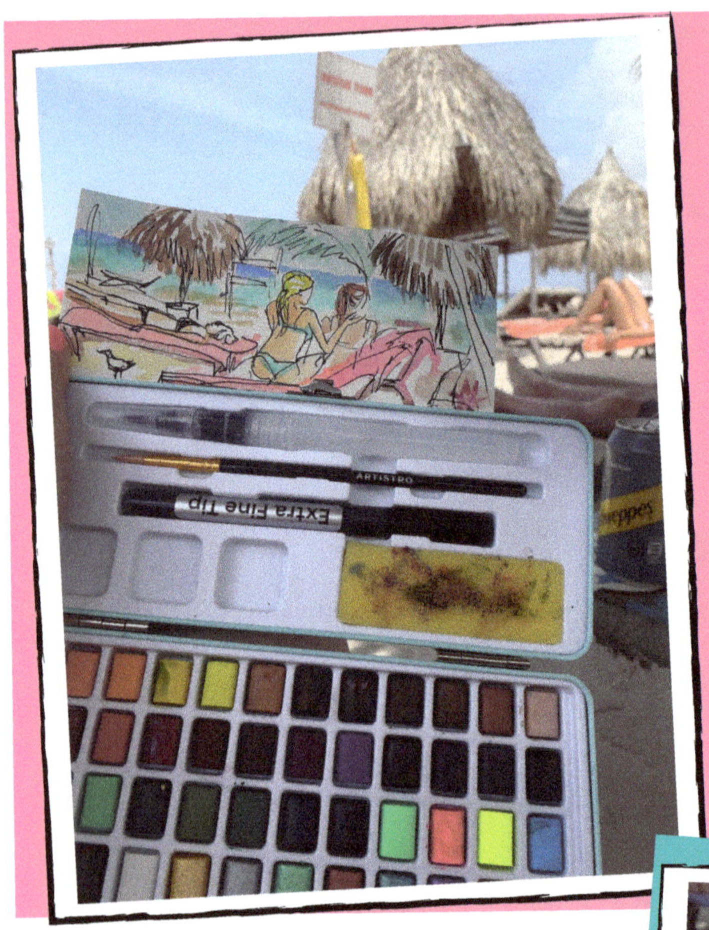

Will you make some mistakes? Sure. Mistakes are a part of learning, and art mistakes can sometimes look interesting and fun. These location sketches are not meant to look or be perfect. They are purely for practice, and, if something cool comes out, it's a bonus.

Squeeze out some water from your watercolor travel brush onto the colors you wish to use from the pallet.

You can wipe off the brush after you're done with a color, to use a new color.
A good tip to remember when drawing on location: Always start with the object closest to you. Like a person or a tree, etc. This establishes the scale for the rest of your scene. Because everything else will be then drawn relative to your largest object in the scene.
All you have to do is position other objects relative to the largest object.

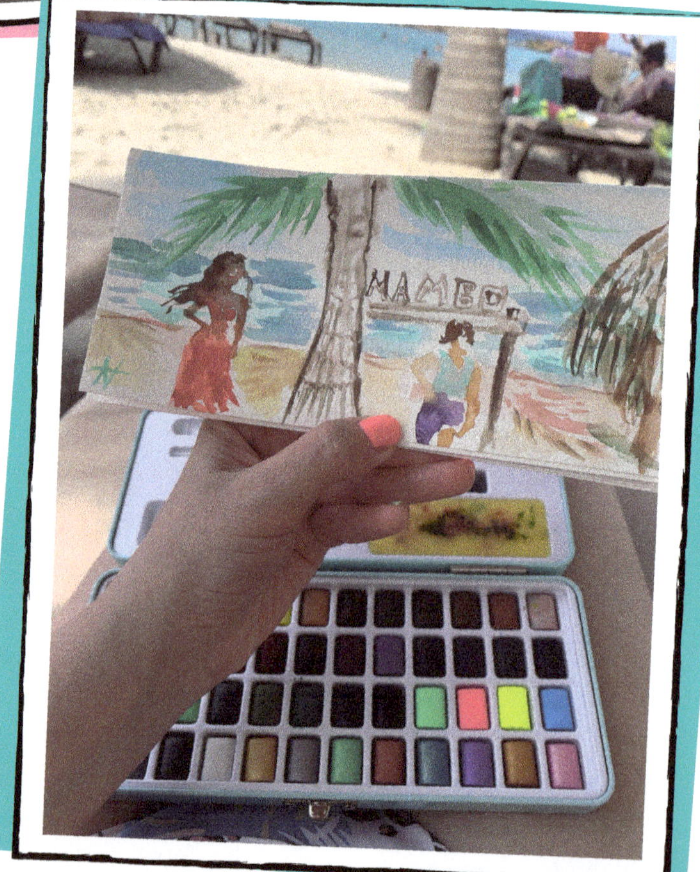

So, next time you go on vacation, don't forget to bring your art supplies with you! Often times, drawings convey the feel of a place even more than photos. Keep traveling and keep drawing!

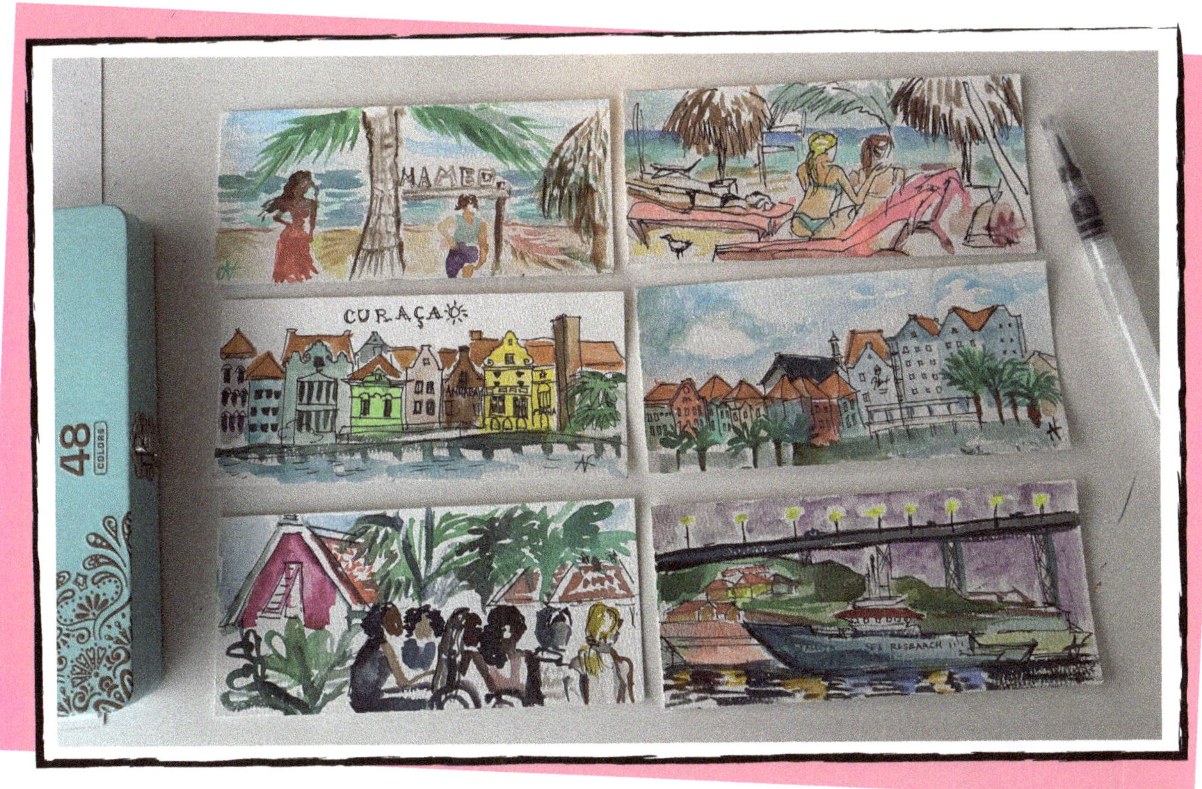

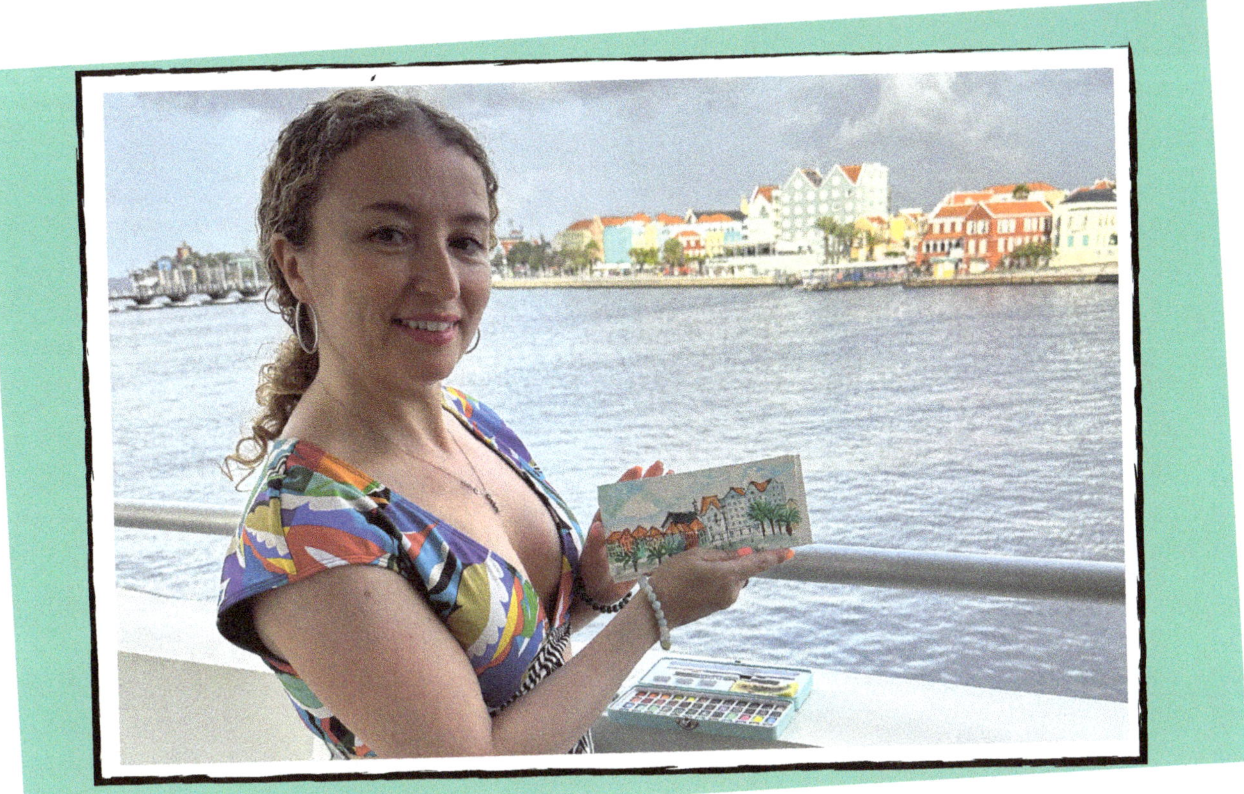

Back to Basics

Finally, let's create a composition using all of the elements we have learned in the book. This composition will comprise of two components. The first would be a simple stylized line of whimsical buildings, drawn in pen. The second will be loose watercolor colorful fashion figures of various scale. The beauty of this exercise is, you can play with positioning your figures in any way that you want, using any color variations. Because our figures are abstract, we don't need to get into details. They still convey what we want them to – loose, stylish and fun fashion figures. Like Pablo Picasso, once we master realistic and detailed scenes, we can more effectively paint and draw stylized and more abstract scenes. We now have the confidence to create something simple, yet compelling. I encourage you to try this, and have fun with it!

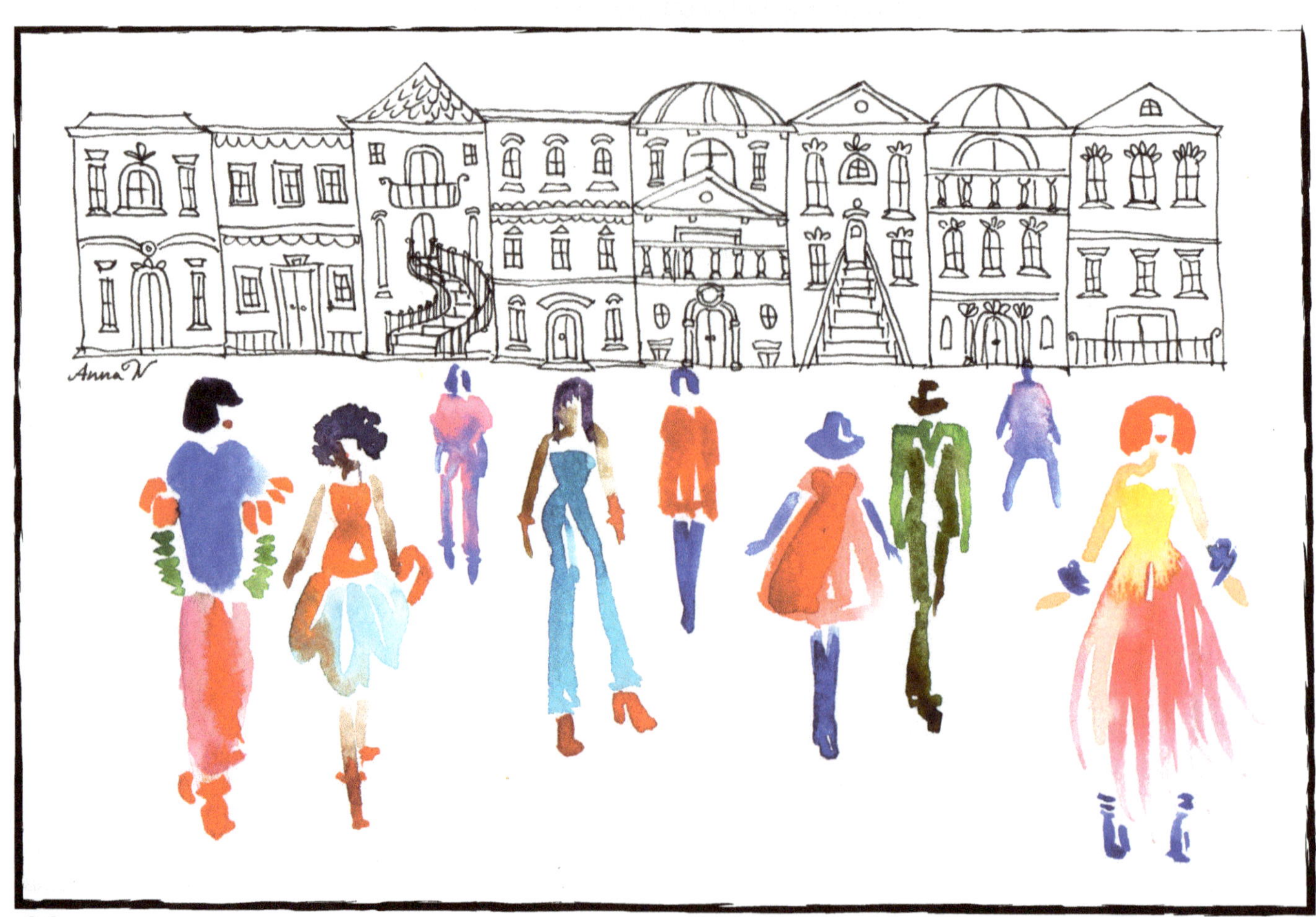

Turn your watercolor paper horizontally, then, at the upper third of the
paper, draw a row of simple yet whimsical houses using your artist pens.
I used 0.5 pen thickness, but you can go thicker or thinner if you prefer.
Draw the houses all the way across your paper. You can copy these:

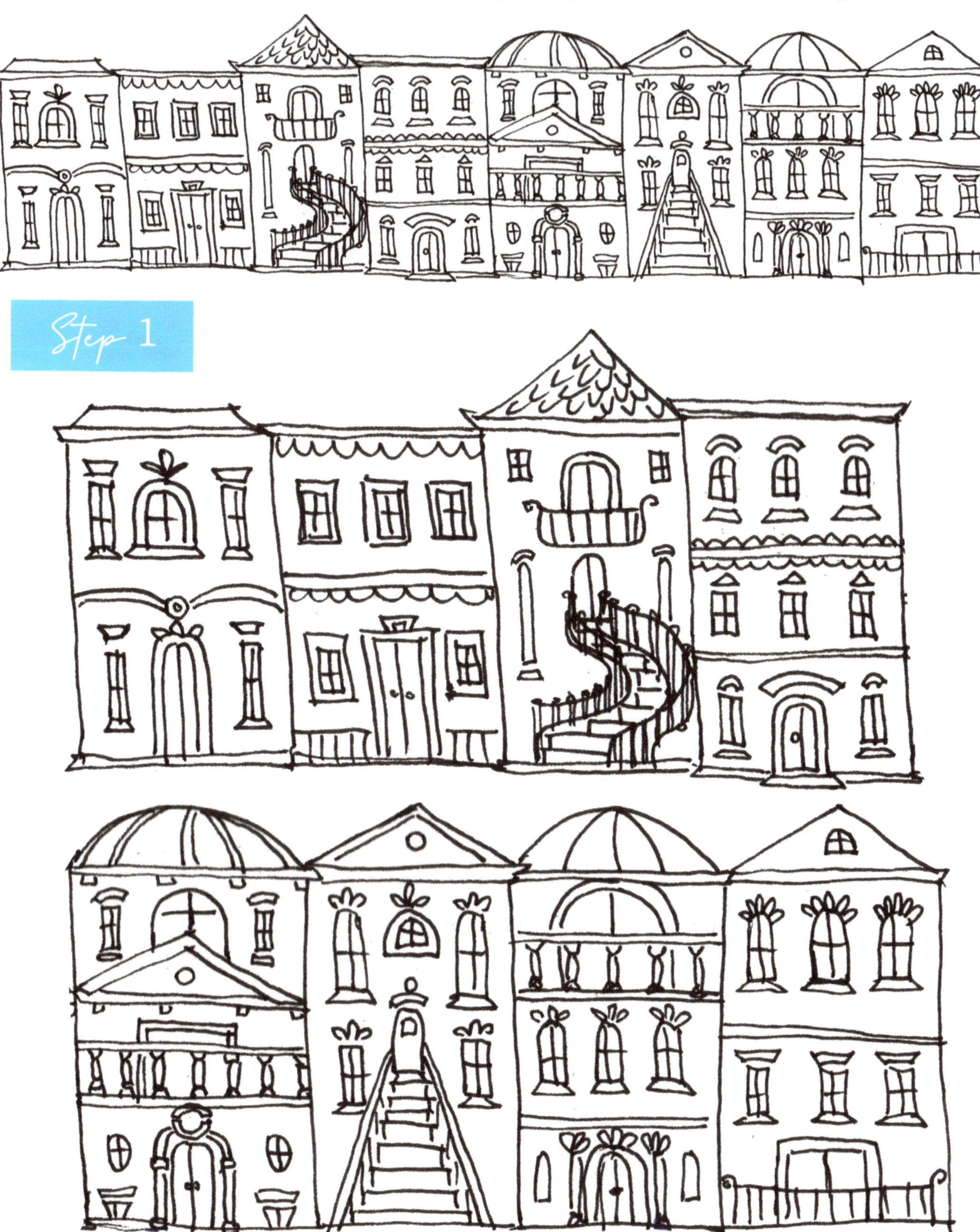

Now let us go to town painting these fun fashion figures! Use loose brush strokes, mixing bright complimentary colors together and sometimes letting them run into one another. Fill up the left side of the page first. To indicate distance, paint some figures smaller, but higher up on the page. Thus they will appear like they are further away.

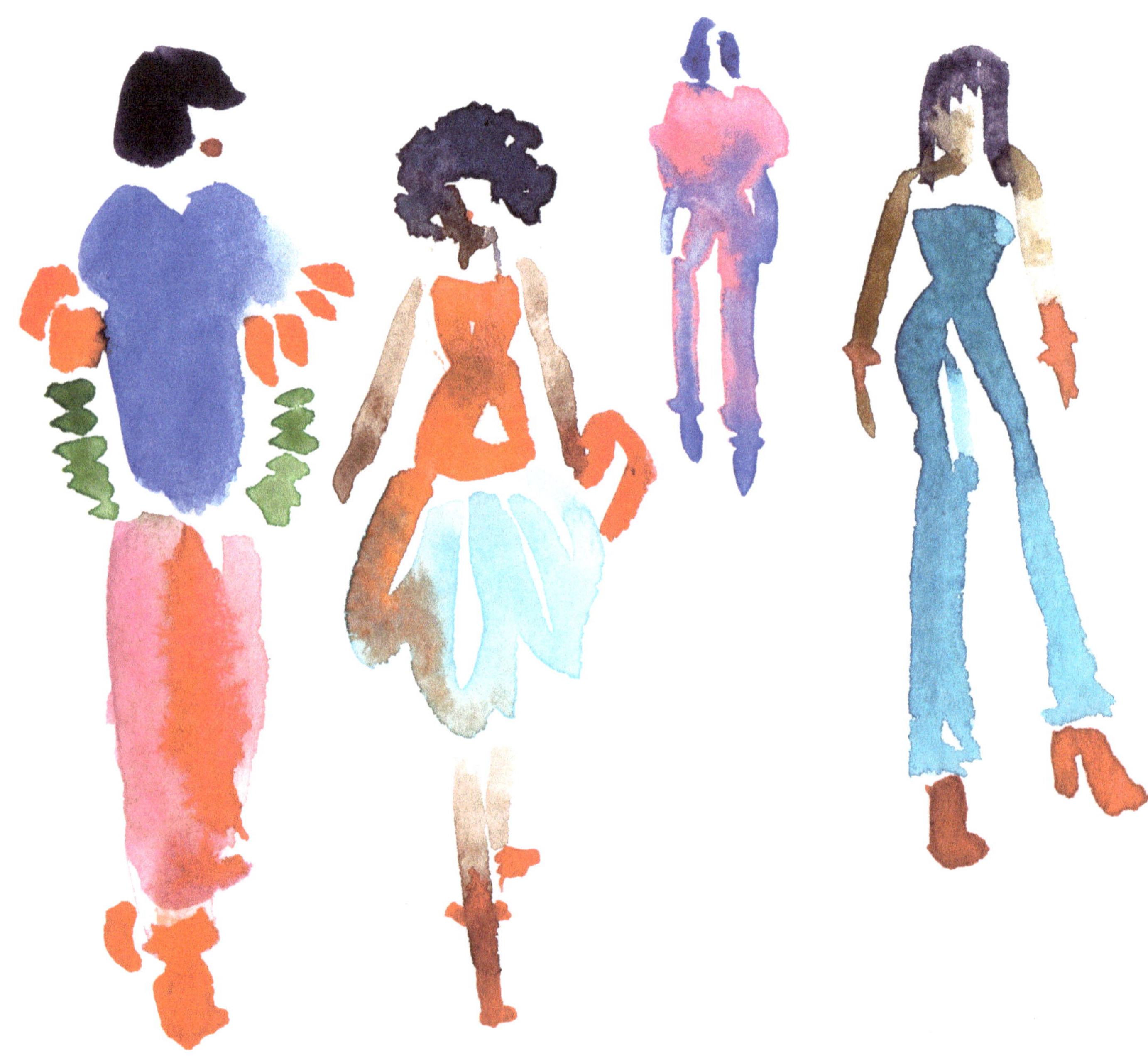

Now continue painting toward the right side of the paper. Note how simple these figures are. You don't have to make them detailed for this exercise. The goal of it is to show how a simple illustration can still convey everything we want, in a bold, expressive and brave way.

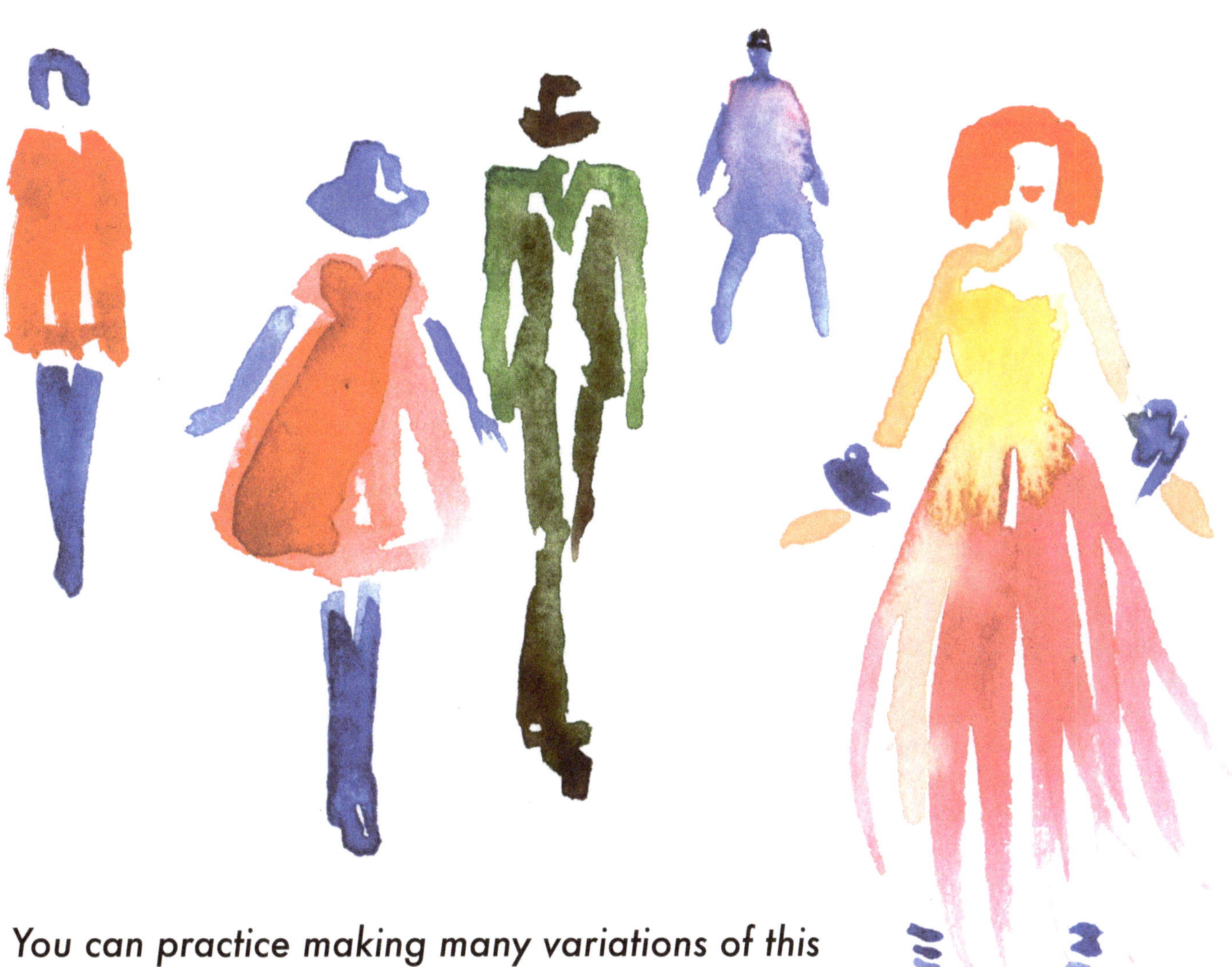

You can practice making many variations of this exercise, by rearranging your figures, experimenting with colors, scale and level of detail. The more you practice, the more interesting and creative your work will turn out!

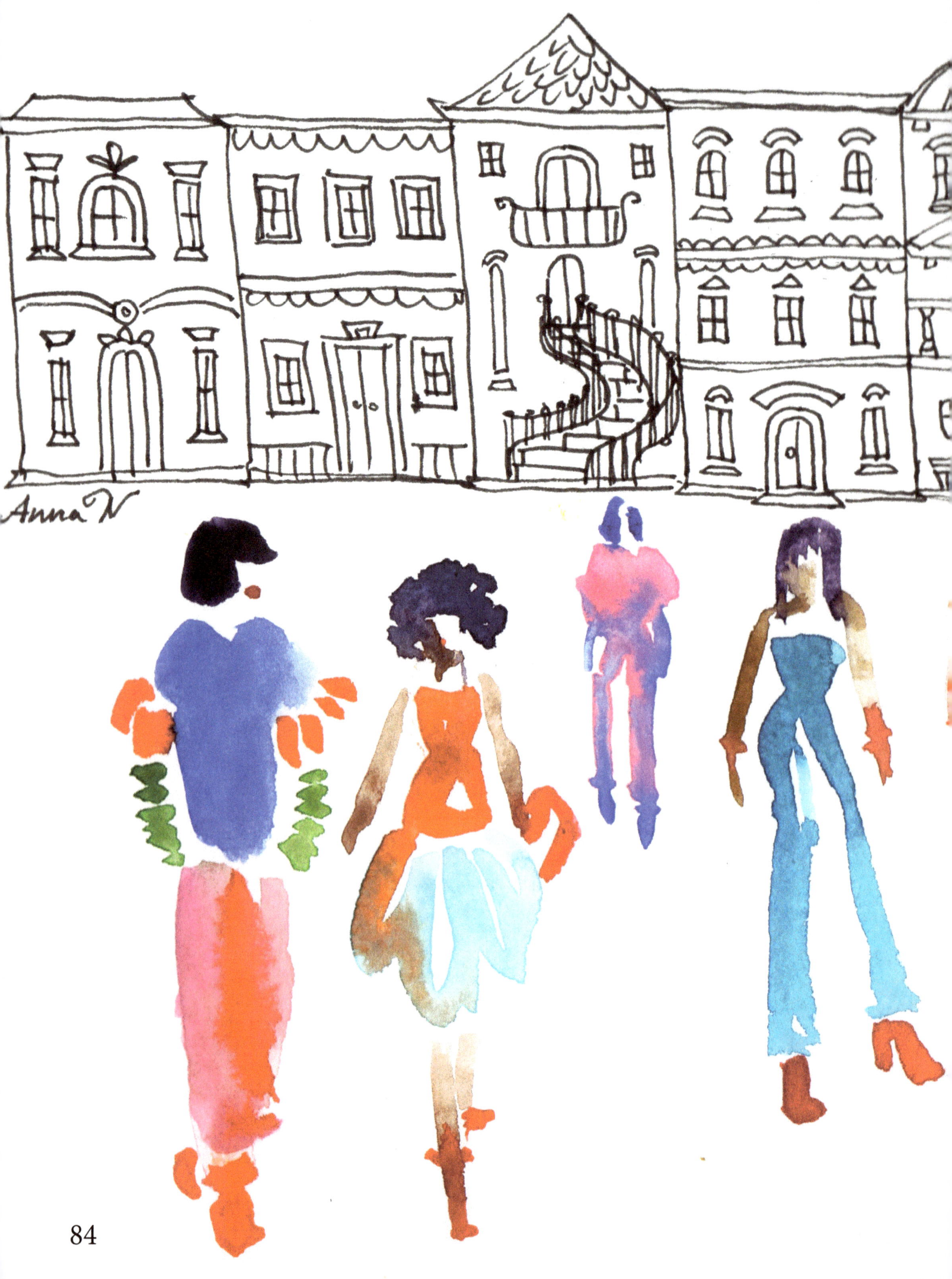
Anna N

Afterword

Thank you for getting this book!

I hope that it has inspired you to take creative freedoms
on your watercolor journey, while learning something new!

You can share what you created by tagging me on Instagram:
@anna_nadler_art

Enjoyed the book? Feel free to leave a review!

Also, check out more books on my website, by scanning the
QR code below, or going to: AnnaNadlerArt.com

Thank you!

Anna